Contents

D1464742

For my Mother-in-Law

THE LATE RENAISSANCE AND MANNERISM

LINDA MURRAY

THAMES AND HUDSON
LONDON

© THAMES AND HUDSON 1967
PRINTED IN ITALY BY ARNOLDO MONDADORI EDITORE

CHAPTER ONE

Michelangelo in Rome

By the 1530s the first phase of the High Renaissance was over. In 1520 Raphael died, and after Giulio Romano went to Mantua in 1524 the Raphael studio broke up; Michelangelo was working in Florence until 1534. Politically, the third decade of the sixteenth century was disastrous. In 1525 Francis I of France was defeated and taken prisoner at the Battle of Pavia, and the French domination of north Italy was replaced by the deadening domination of Spain. In 1527 came the terrible Sack of Rome by the Spanish and German armies of the Emperor Charles V; in the same year the Medici were once more expelled from Florence, but after the Seige of 1529 the city was forced to accept a Medici ruler as Duke. One of the results of the Sack was the dispersal of most of the artists working in Rome. Some, like Sanmicheli and Sansovino, fled to the security and stability of Venice; others, like Rosso, wandered neurotically about, unable to settle after the disaster that had shattered their world. But the stylistic changes that dominate the second half of the century were by no means the result of the upheavals. Far from it: all were inherent in the modifications which Raphael himself had introduced into the style which he had created in Rome between 1510 and 1520. By far the most important of these changes was the search for more decorative, more elaborate, more sophisticated forms, which bit by bit overlaid the rather stark simplicity of the first phase of the High Renaissance, and in the development of these changes Michelangelo played a significant part. His style had always contained a greater degree of complexity than that of any of his contemporaries, and, once Raphael had gone, he dominated Italian art like a Colossus. Only in Venice, as ever resistant to influence from central Italy, was Titian able to maintain independence, although he himself was strongly affected

7

by the more troubled atmosphere that was prevalent there after 1540.

In 1522, the Ghirlandaio fresco of the Resurrection on the entrance wall of the Sistine Chapel was badly damaged, and in 1525 a fire at the altar end of the chapel is thought to have damaged the Perugino frescoes on that wall. The idea of commissioning Michelangelo to paint new frescoes on both these walls seems to have occurred to Clement VII, and the first projects appear to have centred on a 'Resurrection' – a very suitable subject for the altar wall in view of the significance of Jonah above – and a 'Fall of the Rebel Angels' at the entrance. At one time, also, a fresco of the Resurrection was planned for the lunette over the altar of the Medici Chapel, and some drawings by Michelangelo exist which can be associated with this project. Nothing came of either idea for the Sistine Chapel, until it was clear that Michelangelo was not going to stay in Florence. This decision was probably prompted, not only by his revulsion against the new form which Medici rule had taken in Florence, but also by his passionate friendship for Tommaso Cavalieri, a young Roman nobleman whom he had met in 1532, and who fulfilled his ideals of physical beauty, elevated moral character, and intellectual power. For Cavalieri, he made a number of drawings – presentation drawings, not connected with any project in painting or sculpture, and executed in a technique specially invented for the purpose: they are very highly worked in a fine stipple, so that the forms are rather breathed upon the paper than visibly worked with pen or chalk strokes.

Discussions about frescoes in the Sistine Chapel had probably taken place between the Pope and Michelangelo in 1533, during one of his visits to Rome, but as Clement VII died two days after his arrival in 1534, he went back to working on the Tomb. The new Pope, Paul III, was determined that Michelangelo should work for him: he was an old man at the moment of his election, so that time was precious to him. He pursued a policy of fair words and blandishments which was entirely successful; yet it is also clear that he genuinely admired the artist, who returned his feeling.

The first project for a 'Resurrection' seems to have been changed almost imperceptibly from a Resurrection of Christ into a resurrection of the body, of all Christianity, which implies, there-

1 MICHELANGELO *Last Judgement*, 1535-41

fore, a 'Last Judgement'. This choice of subject, while it did not fit in so well with the iconography of the rest of the Chapel, was well suited to the tenor of thought in Rome after the Sack, which was felt to be a divine judgement upon the city and the Church. Michelangelo's treatment of the theme also bears this out, since he abandons the earlier iconography of the subject, in which there is a definite hierarchical division between the saints, the angels, the saved and the damned, in favour of a swirling mass of figures rising to judgement and falling to hell, with the serried ranks of the saints in an accusatory rather than a passively adoring role. Christ Himself is not the impartial Christ of, for example, Giotto's *Last Judgement* in the Arena Chapel, but an angry, menacing figure, the Christ who has suffered for man's sake and who claims the penalty to be exacted for man's contempt of His Sacrifice, while the saints around him brandish the instruments of their martyrdom in a demand for justice. The dead rise from their graves, skeletal, blind-eyed in their newly reborn flesh, stunned, openmouthed in asto-nishment, wonder, horror, fear; they rise in swirling, twisting movement, not in groups but in the isolation of their individual character and fate, all together, yet entirely separate. Below Christ's feet the trumpeters blow with fearful energy, and the pages of the book of life are turned. No Archangel Michael weighs out souls trembling in a balance of good and evil; in this final moment of self-knowledge man knows his fate, and with the realization of his own responsibility, knows himself as the author of his own doom. While the just crowd behind the saints, the wicked throw themsel-ves downwards, away from the sight of God, and falling are driven forward into the mouth of Hell. Above the hosts in heaven are angels bearing the instruments of the passion, turning, tumbling, struggling with cross and column, crown and nails and lance, as if the burden of these things was too great even for the angels to bear. The Virgin here does not attempt her intercessory role; she sits resigned, her head turned away, as if she knew that the moment for pleas for mercy was past, and that only justice re-mained (*Pls. 1, 2*).

Of all the *Last Judgements* of the past, only Signorelli's at Orvieto approaches Michelangelo's in its dramatic character and insight. Where previous painters – and sculptors – had relied on telling

2 MICHELANGELO *Last Judgement*, detail

detail such as the damned dragged to Hell by horrible fantastic
creatures, and the resurrection, and the weighing of souls by
Michael, treated realistically, Signorelli realized that man was more
inhuman and cruel than any fantasy devil, so that his devils in his
Damned in Hell are humans, livid in the colours of decayed and
rotting flesh, but full of the energy and violence that only humans
can bring to the torture of their fellows. Michelangelo has gone
a step further; there are devils, and in human form, grotesque and
horrible, but they are envisaged as man distorted and deformed
by his vices and sins. The real tormentors are not these, however –
they are merely the instruments of man's actions against himself;
the real evil spirits are those who have condemned themselves to
exclusion from communion with God and therefore from fellowship
with the just, and who understand when it is too late what they have
done to themselves. Some of the figures are derived from very
obvious sources. The fulminating Christ is the classical *Jupiter
fulmens*; the devil-boatman driving the damned before him with his
oar is Charon, the ferryman of Hell; the presiding demon is Minos
with his asses ears; the gesture of Niobe sheltering her child becomes Ecclesia receiving the faithful soul; St Catherine holds her

11

wheel as Fortuna drives hers; the trumpeting angels blow like wind-gods. Some figures are the fairly obvious characterizations of the seven deadly sins, or of Despair, but over all these simple re-uses of old ideas, which, by awakening echoes either from outside the limits of Christian interpretation or from earlier representations of Judgement, add to the immediacy of the meaning, are the powerful echoing cadences of the 'Dies irae' and the fearful pleading of the Requiem Mass.

The scaffolding was erected in April 1535, and almost a year was spent preparing the wall, which involved the destruction of the earlier paintings, the pilasters and the cornice, and the filling in of the two windows. Michelangelo had the wall given a slight tilt forwards – a matter of eleven inches in fifty-five feet – in order, as Vasari records, to prevent dust from settling on the painting. At some time, probably in the late sixteenth century, a strip about eighteen inches was obliterated across the width of about forty-three feet at the bottom, so that the altar could be placed higher. Later, prudishness caused many of his nudes to be disfigured by added draperies, some – St Catherine for example, originally entirely nude – to be repainted clothed, but otherwise the fresco is in fairly good condition, except for some chemical changes in the lower part (possibly caused by heat from candles) which have changed light colours to dark and vice versa. Using only one assistant, mainly for the preparation of his colours, Michelangelo worked from the spring of 1535 until the autumn of 1541; the official unveiling was on the Eve of All Saints, 1541 – exactly twenty-nine years after the final unveiling of the ceiling.

Its impact was tremendous. Any work of Michelangelo's was certain not only to reflect current stylistic trends, and sum them up, but also to strengthen – if not anticipate – those aspects of contemporary ideas which fitted in with his personal style. By contrast with the ceiling, the mood is darker, the colour more sombre, the imagery stresses the importance of the nude as the major weapon in his armoury of expression. The conception of the scene is of one vast moving mass of figures, rising and then falling, summoned and impelled by Christ's gesture. The changes of scale, with the figures becoming larger as they rise, until Christ is surrounded by heroic titans, suggests a subjective approach through meaning rather than a purely visual one – though it must be stressed that reproductions that show the vast fresco in small compass distort the effect of these scale changes which, because of perspective, are less striking in the chapel itself. The search for poses expressive of movement and of the emotions inherent in the subject, the deliberate isolation from one another of the figures, each enclosed within his own fate, and the concentration on the nude as the only means of expressing his thought, encouraged other artists to create pictures also dependent on nude figures in twisted, convoluted poses, each figure created more for its effectiveness than for its part in an organic whole. A line can be traced quite clearly from the nude warriors in the *Battle of Cascina*, through the *Adam* and the *Ignudi* of the ceiling, the *Times of Day* of the Medici Tombs, the *Risen Christ* in S. Maria sopra Minerva in Rome (done in the same years as the Medici Chapel), and on to the *Last Judgement*. This development, mixed with the influence of Raphael and Late Antique art, can be seen emerging in other painters – in Vasari and Salviati for instance – as a concentration on the much admired *figura serpentinata*, which rapidly became almost the chief characteristic, and certainly the most striking one, in their works. Michelangelo's *Last Judgement* remained virtually the last word on the subject: Rubens was later to paint a *Fall of the Rebel Angels*, said to be inspired by a design made by Michelangelo for the entrance wall of the chapel but never executed, but no other artist has competed with his cosmic view of the final act of man's earthly career.

The *Last Judgement* was not even finished at the moment when Pope Paul III commissioned the frescoes in the newly built Cappella Paolina. Two frescoes were planned, one on each of the walls flanking the altar niche: the *Conversion of St Paul* (*Pl. 3*) was probably the first to be executed from the autumn of 1542 until the summer of 1545; followed by the *Crucifixion of St Peter* (*Pl. 4*) from March 1546 until 1550 (Paul III died in November 1549). By the time, therefore, that these frescoes were finished Michelangelo was seventy-four, and was also weighed down with his work on St Peter's. Both frescoes share an extraordinary quality of movement. The *Conversion* explodes across the picture, the frightened horse charging into depth, Saul and his immediate helpers falling and fleeing to the left and his other followers flinging themselves to the

3 MICHELANGELO *Conversion of St Paul,* 1542-5

right, while one man stumbles stupidly into the picture at the bottom. Towards this explosive centre, Christ descends like a thunderbolt scattering the angels surrounding Him from his plummeting path, yet He is directed rather upon Saul than upon the void in the centre. Saul, raising himself upon his arm, blinded and semi-conscious, has the tormented face of one who sees more clearly in the dark than he did in the light, and whose conversion is a final acceptance of the divine will travailing in him.

The *Crucifixion of St Peter* shows the moment when the cross is raised and dragged towards the hole prepared for it. Here the movement is circulatory, not with the violent swinging movement of the *Last Judgement,* but with a slow, heavy pace, the plodding action of men who have embarked upon a course without understanding, or even caring, what they do, yet with a foreboding over the consequences expressed in apathy or resignation. The only action is in the group of soldiers, where a centurion points and another allows his horse to rear, yet this movement quickly dies away and the faces of the soldiers express no more than sullen curiosity. No heavenly visions comfort the dying Apostle; he raises his herculean shoulders from the cross and glares out of the fresco, summoning mankind to witness that unflinchingly he pays the debt incurred in that awful moment when the cock crowed, and for which all his life has been a preparation.

Is this the final resignation of an old man, oppressed by age, depressed by the consciousness of increasing infirmity, by the steady growth of his pessimism, his feeling that all mankind is evil, all action bad, or at best useless, and that the only justification is the strength of one's faith? There is no doubt that in the years of his Roman career Michelangelo was closely associated with a group of thinkers advocating reforms in the Church, and imbued

4 MICHELANGELO *Crucifixion of St Peter*, 1546-50

by doctrines which later came to be associated with Protestantism. These much discussed ideas concerning the supreme necessity of faith alone as the means to salvation, later caused some of the group to be pursued as heretics. Vittoria Colonna, who is a central figure in Michelangelo's spiritual life in these years, and who represented for him the most perfect qualities of womanhood, was one of the group that met to discuss the Pauline Epistles in which this doctrine is enshrined. For her he made many drawings (*Pl. 5*), though she seems to have had only a conventional appreciation of art; but her intelligence and the profundity of her religious feeling was such that she had considerable influence over him. The development of his faith, in that it seems at this time to have turned from a normal observance to a deeply reflective piety was largely her work. The course of his spiritual journey can be traced in his poems, for while graceful sonnet-making is quite a normal part of artistic expression – Raphael, for instance, also wrote passable poetry – Michelangelo's poetry is on a par with his art, and forms a perfect gloss upon it. Certain aspects of the *Last Judgement* reflect the ideas that grace is acquired by faith, and faith is the supreme personal achievement of the soul, while sin is the negation of faith, through concentration on purely human qualities which are thereby transformed into vices; and that judgement is not just a judgement of the consequences of sin, but a judgement on the strength, the purity, the essence of the soul's faith, and thereby of its relationship to God. The Pauline frescoes push these ideas a stage further. The original idea for the St Peter fresco was for a 'Giving of the Keys', and it was changed into a martyrdom possibly at the wish of the painter; there is no official record to suggest that it was the Pope who wanted the change, and the two frescoes do not form a natural pair, as the first choice of subjects would have done. But they do express the force of faith: in the *Conversion* the overwhelming impact of faith, which can lead, as the Christian knows, along a long road of suffering and effort to a final martyrdom; in the *Crucifixion*, the moment of martyrdom itself, the culmination and testing point of faith.

Michelangelo's religious thought at the end of his life is also expressed in the last *Pietà* groups (*Pls. 6, 7*). Both are unfinished, both were worked on in his last years, one to within days of his

16

5 MICHELANGELO
Christ on the Cross.
Drawing, *c.* 1541

death in February 1564. Both express the thought of God made Man, and triumphing not by the majesty or power of Godhead, but by the acceptance of suffering and sacrifice, on the same terms, that is, that are open to man for his eventual union with God. The group with Christ upheld by the Virgin and Joseph of Arimathea – whose features are those of the sculptor himself, and who therefore personifies the humanity for whom the sacrifice was made – and lamented over by the Magdalen, now stands as his memorial in Florence Cathedral (*Pl. 6*). This group was being worked on in the 1550s, but Michelangelo, dissatisfied with it because the block was flawed, and because he was importuned to finish it, smashed it in a fit of rage and frustration. One of his assistants pieced it together and finished the Magdalen. The second group, the Rondanini *Pietà* (*Pl. 7*), seems to have been worked twice over, once with a Christ slumped forward but held almost upright by the

6 MICHELANGELO *Pietà*,
late 1550s

Virgin, and then again as a figure almost melting into the body
of the supporting Virgin. What happened to the original conception and the first state of the block can only be surmised from
its present state: it is an expression of the most profound pathos,
heightened by its unfinished state, in which the forms are barely
sketched in, and the two bodies seem to merge one into the other.
In the form these last works take, and in the emotion they express,
Michelangelo comes very close to Donatello's final pulpits, and in
turn Titian, Rembrandt and Cézanne are his companions in old age.

In 1546 Antonio da San Gallo the Younger died. The main works
occupying him at the end of his life were the Farnese Palace (*Pl. 8*),
built for the papal family, and St Peter's. The palace was the largest

7 MICHELANGELO
Rondanini Pietà,
worked on until 1564

and grandest in Rome, a hundred feet high by about two hundred feet wide, a free-standing block on a site stretching down to the Tiber. In 1545 Michelangelo won a competition for the design for the cornice, much to San Gallo's mortification, and after his death completed the palace. The problem with the cornice was to design one proportionate to the bulk of the whole building, but which should not appear to crush the upper storey. Michelangelo's solution was to increase the height of the top floor, so that the cornice was lifted well above the window pediments, and thus appeared to float above the whole. He also built the top storey of the courtyard much higher than the arcaded loggie below, and introduced the complications in levels in the pilasters of the order and of the framing elements in the windows themselves, so that the storey is richly decorative and strikingly different from the sober massiveness of the arcades below with their infilling of simply pedimented windows. His first purely architectural work in Rome continues directly, therefore, from the wealth of complicated layers and mouldings of the Medici Chapel. The great window in the façade, too, he redesigned so that it tells as a void, wider and apparently tightly clamped between the columns framing it.

He was appointed architect to St Peter's from January 1547, and immediately set about redesigning the basilica (*Pl. 10*). At Raphael's death in 1520, the plan of the church had been altered to make a long nave, but Bramante's pupil Peruzzi had prepared designs based on Bramante's own reworking of his original Greek cross plan, simplified and with larger central piers. Antonio da San Gallo compromised; he returned to the central plan in a somewhat condensed form, but added to it a large vestibule in front to contain a benediction loggia (*Pl. 11*). The model for his project still exists (*Pl. 9*). It is an extraordinary compendium of practically every known architectural form: arcades, colonnades, variously pedimented windows, orders of pilasters, an enormous dome with a multi-layer colonnaded drum like a Milanese *tiburio*, smaller domes, lanterns, towers, an enormous void in the centre for the loggia and a straggling irregular outline. Many years before, when Michelangelo was painting the Sistine Ceiling, there had been no love lost between himself and Bramante; however, faced with the same problem as his predecessor he recognized the basic rightness of Bramante's

8 SAN GALLO Farnese Palace, courtya

inspiration. 'It cannot be refuted', he wrote, 'that Bramante was as able in architecture as any man since antiquity. He laid down the first plan for St Peter's, not full of confusion, but clear and precise, luminous and free-standing, so that it did not impair the palace, and was considered a beautiful thing, as is still manifest; so that whoever departs from Bramante's plans, as San Gallo has done, departs from the truth...' Michelangelo also objected to San Gallo's design that it was dark inside, and would be unnecessarily expensive to build. He proposed to return to a central plan, much simpler than Bramante's since the minor Greek cross elements in the four corners would be replaced by a grand ambulatory encircling much enlarged central piers. The internal space was envisaged as flowing in such a way that it defined the basic square of the plan, while the projecting apses and the subsidiary enclosed spaces flanking them would, on the outside, create that modulation of shape essential to give movement to the great entablature, and variety of size to the bay system of the giant pilasters. In this

way, the mass of the building would become an interesting and vital block as a podium for the dome. The façade was to be a large colonnaded portico, with a pediment, though this leaves the problem of the benediction loggia unsolved. The whole was to be surmounted by an hemispherical dome, encircled on the upper drum by a colonnade of coupled columns framing pedimented windows.

He built most of the exterior on the north and south, though the western apse was hardly started, and his dome had only reached the top of the colonnaded drum when he died (*Pl. 13*). Unfortunately, he did not lay out the façade, so that when he was dead it was possible to revive the long-nave project, and to extend the front of the building with unhappy consequences for the proportions of his dome. The parts that he did complete consist in the main of a giant order of pilasters, multi-layered on framing strips, bearing an enormous entablature and surmounted by a high attic storey, with short pilaster-like elements corresponding to the giant order below. The bays framed by these pilasters contain huge tabernacle windows of very varied shape, two large ones in the main bays and four smaller openings in the narrow bays, and the attic also has windows varying in size and shape. Some are true windows, lighting the interior, others are blind niches, serving only a decorative function; but all through he has been concerned to compose new forms and combinations inspired by the language of classical architecture, so as to extend it for modern purposes. This is a further instance of the point Vasari made in connection with the Laurenziana: Michelangelo never imitates the antique, but creates on a par with it.

During the years when the structure was being built, Michelangelo considered the problems presented by the dome. In July 1547 he wrote to his nephew Lionardo in Florence for detailed information about Brunelleschi's dome, and it seems that at one time he considered making the lantern octagonal in shape, like that of Florence Cathedral. Also, the final execution of the dome, by his pupil Giacomo della Porta between 1585 and 1590, on a pointed profile instead of the original idea of an hemisphere, is not without foundation in Michelangelo's own alternative projects. Dupérac, the French engraver and architect, who was in Rome from 1559 until well after Michelangelo's death, and who published a series of

9 SAN GALLO Model for St Peter's

engravings of St Peter's, shows the dome as hemispherical, but
otherwise much as it was eventually built (*Pl. 12*). However, in
view of Maderno's later lengthening of the nave, the heightening
was just as well, for the present dome has difficulty in dominating
the façade, seen from the Piazza, though it floats superbly, effort-
lessly, from a distance. One of Michelangelo's prime considerations
was the buttressing of this massive cupola; he had before him,
always, the example of the Pantheon, an hemispherical dome 142
feet across, apparently entirely unbuttressed. He also had in mind
Brunelleschi's *cupolone* for Florence cathedral, very pointed, octagonal, and strengthened at the bottom by the lobes of choir and
transepts and by the exedrae between them. Bramante's inspiration
had been to raise the 'dome of the Pantheon upon the arches of the

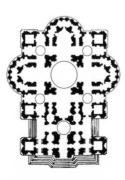

10 (*left*) DUPÉRAC Michelangelo's plan for St Peter's,
c. 1547. Engraving, 1568
11 (*right*) SAN GALLO
Plan for St Peter's

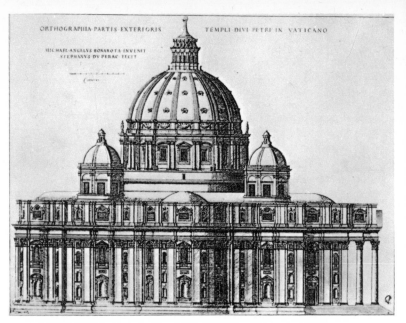

12 DUPÉRAC Engraving of Michelangelo's project for St Peter's

Temple of Peace' (that is, the basilica of Constantine); Michelangelo clearly believed that visible buttressing would be a regressive form, since none of his drawings ever shows any, and the recurrent enlargement of the central piers shows that this inspiration had dominated all the architects of the basilica, except San Gallo. In fact, the dome is borne by the gigantic piers as its main support, though they, of course, receive considerable strength from the structures which abut on them. Some idea of the dimensions of this church can be obtained from one comparison: St Paul's in London, which is 365 feet high outside, would fit inside St Peter's, whose interior dome is 370 feet from the floor, and all eight of Wren's massive piers would fit into one of St Peter's.

Upon St Peter's he laboured until the end of his life, working for nothing, since he considered it as an offering to God. Other architectural commissions undertaken included the redesigning of the Capitoline Hill, the designing of a new entrance gate to the city, the Porta Pia, though this was largely built by his assistants, the abortive designs for the Florentine church in Rome, S. Giovanni dei Fiorentini, and for the mother church for the Jesuit Order,

13 MICHELANGELO View of the apse and dome of St Pet

which he offered to build for St Ignatius Loyola, whom he knew personally. S. Maria degli Angeli was built from 1561 onwards out of the remaining tepidarium of the Baths of Diocletian for a convent of Carthusians; unfortunately, it was so reconstructed and redecorated by Vanvitelli in 1749 that little of Michelangelo's rather gaunt church survives but the general form, the articulation of enormous antique columns, and the sailing quality of the vaults, which are the original Roman vaults repaired. The funerary chapel for the two Sforza cardinals in S. Maria Maggiore was his last essay in interpenetrating volumes. Here three systems of vaulting occur: a quadripartite vault above the main space, apsidal ribbed domes over the shallow niches containing the tombs, and a semi-circular barrel vault over the altar; these disparate spaces are held together visually by strongly projecting angles with huge columns, and the interior is executed with plain plaster and travertine stone, usually only used for exteriors. He had also, in 1550-51, rebuilt Bramante's witty and amusing semi-circular stair at the end of the Vatican Belvedere. The niche was rebuilt as a two-storey structure with a

suite of rooms, the space being taken on the courtyard side which meant that the stairs had to go. Michelangelo's flight is like that designed for the front of the Senate, and the top terrace was used, about 1615, for the antique Pine Cone formerly in the atrium of Old St Peter's.

The redesigning of the Capitoline Hill, the focal point of Roman political history, going back to the Caesars and looking outwards across the city towards the conquered world, required long and detailed planning. Under the Senate were – are still – the remains of the Tabularium or Archives, and on the high point to the north is S. Maria in Aracoeli, built on the top of the Tarpeian Rock, the foundation rock of Rome. A palace for a lay legislature had been built on the south side of the raggedly open space of the Campidoglio in the fifteenth century, but until Paul III initiated the new works in 1537 almost nothing had been done to give secular Rome the kind of civic centre that all self-respecting Italian cities by then possessed. This was because, despite figure-head senators, the seat of true government was in the Vatican; when the Senate was erected on the antique ruins, and the statue of Marcus Aurelius moved from the Lateran, both were made to look across the empty waste towards new Rome, instead of across the Forum.

Except for designing the new base for the equestrian statue placed in the centre of the piazza, which must have involved some replanning of the whole square, Michelangelo was not closely concerned with the project until after 1547; he would not collaborate with anybody from San Gallo's 'clan', as he called them. Between

15 DUPÉRAC Michelangelo's design for the Capitoline Hill. Engraving

1547 and 1612, work proceeded slowly but steadily. Michelangelo's designs for the piazza consisted of an ordered façade for the Senate, two palaces to north and south, a grand stairway up the hillside to the piazza, and a carefully designed pattern in the paving like a radiating star with three stressed points directed at the main egresses from the piazza. Also, the two palaces – the Conservatori on the south (*Pl. 14*), and the Capitoline on the north – were to be so aligned that the square narrowed towards the steps. This not only fitted the existing structures, but reinforced the enclosed quality of the space. The present Senate only retains from Michelangelo's original design the use of a giant order and the lowest storey treated as a basement against which the double flights of the grand staircase were placed; the present stair is without the important projecting portico at the top, and has a fountain below instead of the antique River Gods which he intended to incorporate. For the Conservatori (virtually the town-hall of Rome) he designed a front consisting of a giant order bearing a huge entablature and cornice, with a balustrade over it; the bays of the façade between the giant pilaster have an open loggia below and a series of grand windows above – solid over void, that is. Each opening of the

27

MICHELANGELO Conservatori Palace, designed *c.* 1539

loggia is framed in an order of columns, the entablature of which forms the base upon which rests the order framing the great window above, so that a lesser order is enclosed within a greater one; the giant pilasters are backed by framing elements so that his usual layering device is also present. On the back wall of the loggia large pedimented doorways correspond to the row of windows in the upper storey; the pediments alternate – all segmental above enclosing large shells, all triangular below, and these doors are set between columns responding to the order on the outside of the loggia, so that every part of the design contributes to a coherent whole. After Michelangelo's death, the Campidoglio, like St Peter's, was also finished by della Porta. No complete designs for the Senate seem ever to have been made, and Dupérac's 1568 engraving appears to be derived from sketches and possible statements of intention (*Pl. 15*); della Porta changed the staircase by omitting the baldaquin or portico at the top, and finished the façade on his own initiative; he also built the central window of the Conservatori, which was probably planned to be the same size as the others, and over the huge opening he placed a triangular pediment jammed tightly between the framing pilasters; and he altered the paving pattern to a mundane radiating spoke system, with four entrance points stressed. This has now been relaid with Michelangelo's radiating star pattern – a still centre enclosing the symbol of power, yet one from which power radiates. The return bays at the ends of the Conservatori were doubled, making the block from the side look like a truncated palace façade instead of a loggia; the Capitoline palace opposite was not built until the seventeenth century.

Basically, Michelangelo's architecture is sculpture, in that he models the units as if they were free-standing statues, and the elements as if they were the limbs and features of a figure. He concentrates on movement, on a sense of tension and vitality, and every element no matter how small contributes to the enrichment of the surface, and to the contrasts of void and solid, light and shadow. He is endlessly inventive, in planning, in his detail, and in his sense of proportion, and the freedom with which he created a whole vocabulary of new architectural forms was of vital consequence not only to his contemporaries and successors, but also well into the Baroque.

28

CHAPTER TWO

Mannerism

Raphael's large workshop contained one major artist: Giulio Romano. He grew up virtually in the studio, and became Raphael's chief assistant at about the time of the Stanza dell'Incendio – that is, about 1515 or 1516. The point at which he first appears is a problem largely governed by his age at his death in 1546. The hospital record of his death says that he was forty-seven, which makes him born in 1499. Two lines of argument are then open; either he was an infant prodigy, able to create independently from about the age of sixteen, or else the hospital record (which is probably based on a statement by his widow) is wrong, and Vasari, who knew him, was nearer the truth when he places his birthdate in 1492. If Vasari is right, he would have been about twenty-three when he is first identifiable as a distinct personality in Raphael's studio. Much of the change in Raphael's art, towards stronger chiaroscuro, less centralized compositions, greater movement and emotional expression in the figures, which appears after the Stanza della Segnatura, has been associated with Giulio, as if the pupil rather than the master had been in control. It is absurd to suggest that he introduced these features, particularly since they appear in the *Heliodorus*, which, if 1499 is the right birthdate, would make him a major influence on Raphael at the age of fifteen. It is more reasonable to suppose that Giulio followed Raphael's development, which, from about the time of the Tapestry Cartoons and the Stanza dell'Incendio, tended towards those features which, commonly, are associated with the development of Mannerism.

Mannerism is a term requiring rather careful definition, for unlike Early or High Renaissance, and, later, Baroque, it cannot be equated strictly with a period and used as an equivalent and defining label for all the works produced in a specific time bracket.

It is a much more selective definition, for it is a label only for certain works of a certain kind produced by certain artists between about 1520 and 1590, and only in certain parts of Italy. The term itself was invented in the 1920s because the old divisions of High Renaissance and Baroque left a large body of sixteenth-century Italian art which could not properly be included under either head without making stylistic nonsense of both definitions. The perfectly sound time-label of Late Renaissance exists in German and would, indeed, be a far better denomination for the art produced after 1520 than has resulted from the blanket use of the term Mannerist. Recent years have seen determined efforts to define Mannerism more narrowly, but this is rendered difficult unless it can be entirely divorced from its period connection and confined to style, as has, in fact, partially occurred with the confusing back-formation of 'Quattrocento Mannerism' used sometimes to describe certain aspects of Botticelli and Filippino. In its artistic context the term originates with Vasari (it is in common usage very much earlier in literary and social contexts), who uses '*maniera*' as an equivalent of 'style' in its absolute sense (... in the style of...), and in the figurative sense as a qualitative judgement (... in a beautiful style...), in which sense it is allied with '*grazia*' an omnibus term for grace, beauty, lightness, charm, pleasingness, spontaneity, and a host of other desirable aesthetic equivalents of those social qualities that Castiglione, in 'The Courtier', deems essential for good manners and conduct. Later, probably because the term degenerated somewhat socially, and came to be equated with artificiality of behaviour and displeasing affectation, seventeenth-century criticism – notably Bellori – regarded *maniera* as an undesirable quality, inimical to the true representation of nature. It is in this sense that Vasari's application of *maniera* came to be used as a description of the kind of style which he himself practised, and which the seventeenth century clearly, and rightly, saw was a development from the late style of Raphael and characteristic of a particular type of art produced in Rome and Florence after 1520.

Mannerism can be quite easily recognized and defined: in general it is equated with a concentration on the nude, often in bizarre and convoluted poses, and with exaggerated muscular development; with subject matter either deliberately obscure, or treated

so that it becomes difficult to understand – the main incident pushed
into the background or swamped in irrelevant figures serving as
excuses for displays of virtuosity in figure painting; with extremes
of perspective, distorted proportions or scale – figures jammed into
too small a space so that one has the impression that any movement
would burst the confines of the picture space; with vivid colour
schemes, employing discordant contrasts, effects of 'shot' colour,
and the use of colour, not for descriptive or naturalistic purposes,
but as a powerful adjunct to the emotional impact of a picture.
In architecture, it concentrates on violations of the rules governing
accepted usage of the classical orders, and on irrational and un-
predictable dispositions of space, combinations of features, treatment of surfaces. It is invariably accompanied by rich decoration,
and often by elaborate illusionism. In sculpture, it is discerned in the
change from High Renaissance frontality and simplicity of presentation to a search for multiplicity of views and silhouette, elongation of forms, and exaggerated effects of perspective and scale in
reliefs. A Mannerist statue must be walked round, for all its angles
of view are equally important. But it is quite clear that this definition
cannot possibly describe all the works of art produced during the
greater part of the sixteenth century, even in Rome and Florence,
which are the true homes of Mannerism; there is a very great deal
that escapes the net. It is almost totally inapplicable to Venice and
its province, except where an individual artist – such as Porde-
none – deliberately cultivated Mannerist characteristics and used
them as forms of Grand Manner painting to impress provincial
patrons, with, one suspects, the intention to *'épater le bourgeois'*.
Neither is it a consistent quality within the *œuvre* of an artist:
for instance, Salviati's grandiose *Triumph* frescoes in the Palazzo
Vecchio in Florence, painted 1545-8, are not Mannerist in the sense
that this term can be applied to his slightly later frescoes in the
Palazzo Farnese in Rome (*Pl. 36*). Bronzino, who is one of the
most relentless practitioners of the style in his figure paintings,
sometimes carries the characteristics into his portraits, but by no
means always.

In painting the style implies a deliberate derivation from late
Raphael and from Michelangelo's *Last Judgement* and the Cappella
Paolina frescoes; in architecture, from Michelangelo again, in the

31

Medici Chapel, the Laurenziana, and the Roman works, and also from Raphael's late palaces and the Villa Madama; in sculpture, by extension from Michelangelo's paintings in which the figures are, so to speak, conceived as sculpture in a single plane, and from antique sculpture 'Raphaelized'. Few of Michelangelo's figures except perhaps the *Risen Christ*, one of his less successful works which he declared to have been spoilt by an assistant, have the all-round quality, though the *Moses* of the Tomb, and the *Slaves* now in the Louvre are not absolutely frontal. When the term Mannerist comes to be applied outside Italy, then its accuracy of definition is slightly blurred. It implies, for its full impact, a knowledge of what had gone before – of the High Renaissance, in fact – and this is particularly true of the architecture. The point of Mannerist architecture is in its violations of the High Renaissance and classical forms and canons; for countries whose preceding architectural style was Gothic, the whole point is lost. Northern Mannerism exists, but it is not the same kind of thing; it is the imitation of Italian forms of the mid- to late-sixteenth century in the north because they were new, fashionable, and expressive of a freshly acquired culture. That the most imitated forms happened to be Mannerist ones is because they were the most recent to evolve in Italy, and also more sensationally obvious.

While Raphael lived, Giulio's artistic personality was naturally somewhat obscured by his master's fame and responsibility for work executed in the studio. It is by working backwards from his achievements after Raphael's death that he emerges with distinct characteristics that differentiate him from Raphael: rather fat forms, strongly modelled in a heavy chiaroscuro, expressive heads and gestures tending towards the over-emphatic, turgid colour with inky shadows, congested compositions built up in layers, but with sudden, unexpected plunges into a distant vista, seen through a door or between columns. Even where his entire responsibility seems certain, as in parts of the Farnesina decoration, or in the Stanza dell'Incendio, there is also evidence that Raphael never completely relaxed his control, so that Giulio's forms reflect ideas that Raphael himself held. After 1520 he completed the *Transfiguration* (which was sufficiently far forward to be exhibited over Raphael's bier, as Vasari recounts), and the Sala di Costantino,

16 GIULIO ROMANO Sala di Costantino, *Baptism of Constantine*, 1520-24

the last of the sequence of Stanze where Raphael's Roman career had begun, is entirely by him (*Pl. 16*). The frescoes, dedicated to the history of the early Church, present several novelties; whereas the Raphael Stanze had been painted round the windows and doors clearly upon wall surfaces, the Sala di Costantino takes over the Farnesina device of the awning and transfers it to the walls, turning the pictures into fictive tapestries. Between them are pedestals supporting fictive statues at the base of which sit allegorical figures of Virtues, and all the way round underneath runs an elaborate dado painted with scenes in grisaille. The fake tapestry device may also have been suggested by the tapestries hung in the Sistine Chapel; there is, too, the example of illusionism in the Sistine Ceiling, where

33

fictive architecture is inhabited by figures and interspersed by painted bronze medallions and statues of *putti*. As a treatment for very large walls it has the advantage of breaking up the decoration into sections of reasonable size. It was a device with a great future. The scenes themselves contain the now customary mixtures of heroic narratives set amid a large cast of attendant supporting figures – mothers and children, beggars, dogs, exclamatory bystanders, dwarfs, pages – all arranged in beautiful poses. Two scenes have elaborate architectural settings. One is a modified view of the Lateran Baptistery: the other is an idealized view of Old St Peter's, which, however, may contain a good deal of truth about the *confessio* and apse, for in 1524 parts of the Constantinian basilica still stood. The *Battle at the Milvian Bridge* is the next great battle scene after Leonardo's abortive one in Florence, and the struggling mass of men and horses in the centre possibly reflects the prototype which Raphael himself would have known, and which would certainly have been known also to Penni, the Florentine assistant whom Giulio inherited from Raphael. In 1524 Giulio decided to accept the long-standing invitations of the Gonzaga, and moved to Mantua, leaving the Sala di Costantino unfinished, but with designs ready for assistants to complete. His decision to leave Rome may have been prompted by the scandal over a set of illustrations to Aretino's immoral verses, for which he is said to have made the drawings. Be that as it may, he journeyed with Castiglione to Mantua, where he spent the rest of his life, converting the city from a swampy backwater into a place filled with palaces and set about with splendid ducal villas. Little now survives, for most of the architecture was in brick with stucco surfaces, there being no stone locally, and damp and neglect have completed the ravages that wars began.

His great surviving monument is the Palazzo del Tè just outside the town on what was then an island occupied by the stables of the most famous stud in Europe (*Pls. 17, 18*). It was not built as a place to live in, but as a classical *villa suburbana* to be used for festivities. It is a single storey building round a square court, with a great garden ending in an exedra, reached across a moat that served as fishponds. Each façade is pierced by a loggia, so that the palace has two axes, one leading through from the original main entrance (the present main entrance was not designed as such) into the gar-

17 GIULIO ROMANO
Courtyard of the
Palazzo del Tè,
1526 onwards

den, and the other ending in a blank wall at the back of the south
side, where the façade was never finished. As one approaches the
villa one thing is immediately clear: this is not a repetitious arrangement of bays about a central doorway, but a balance of contrasts,
with a tense conflict between enormous rough keystones and heavily rusticated windows and doorways clasped between smoothly
surfaced pilasters – giant pilasters, embracing in their short, stumpy
form the main storey and the mezzanine above, with a plain string-
course running behind them like a ribbon threaded through from
one end to the other. The order is very plain Tuscan Doric, with
rusticated bases formed in the stucco, like masses of wriggling
worms. Inside the main door (the original west one) – a colonnaded
and coffered barrel-vaulted tunnel to the courtyard – another
curious device is met with: the columns on either side are only
roughly hewn, not smoothly finished as they should be, but en-

35

18 GIULIO ROMANO Loggia of the Palazzo del Tè

closed in a muff of rough 'stone' (only they are made of stucco)
to suggest a half-finished appearance. This is a parody of the great
vestibule of the Palazzo Farnese in Rome, a slightly pretentious
joke to ape the splendours but only to do it by halves. The west
façade, with the triple arched entrance, is split down the centre
with an almost solid wall, so that the two halves of the loggia are
quite separate, one looking outwards, originally across the water to
the city, the other inwards to the court. On the garden front, the
loggia opens splendidly like the one at the Villa Madama which
Giulio had helped to decorate: from the garden side three great
arches borne on blocks of four columns give into a barrel vaulted
space, decorated entirely with the type of relief plaster and painted
decoration derived from Nero's Golden House which had been the
inspiration for the Villa Madama. Here all is lightness and delicacy,
gay, frivolous almost, and infinitely graceful, for the façade to the

19 GIULIO ROMANO Sala dei Giganti, Palazzo del Tè, 1532

garden is a sequence of these arches, not equally spaced, but all variations on the theme of the antique motive later to be called the Palladian motive. Turn back from the loggias into the courtyard and the full force of the contrasts strikes one: this is a building turned inside out, for the court has thunderous, fortress forms, heavy columns clinging to the rusticated walls, framing deep niches and pedimented blind windows, and supporting a Doric entablature where the triglyphs are slipping loosely and dangerously from the frieze so that on one side the order appears to be broken and ruinous. Inside is a long sequence of variously shaped rooms, with elaborate ceilings and mosaic floors, some ceilings coffered, some painted, one room devoted to the glories of the stud, others to fanciful mythologies, and, in the Sala di Psyche, the story of Psyche treated so as to be highly suited to the licence and moral freedom which it was one of the objects of the villa to serve. In the far corner of the long enfilade of rooms, Giulio devised a surprise: the Sala dei Giganti (*Pl. 19*) is ill-lit – purposely – so that the paintings on the walls are the more astonishing. In the centre of the coved ceiling is the temple of Jove, supported on clouds, while Jove himself surrounded by the affrighted gods and goddesses of Olympus hurls down his thunderbolts upon the presumptuous Titans who tried to storm the sacred mountain, and who lie crushed under

the weight of temples and rocks tumbling about them in a cataclysmic earthquake. Originally, a shattered fireplace blended perfectly with the falling rocks so that its flames added their reality to the fictions on the walls, and the floor of carefully set pebbles masked the point where the decoration began. This is the epitome of Mannerist decoration – this blend of the real and the false, of the witty, sophisticated and amusing in the imagery with the seriousness of the moral content of the myth, the contrast between the consciousness of the solidity of reality and the imaginativeness of the terrifying carnage on the walls.

Giulio's only assistant of merit in the Tè was Primaticcio, who was with him for five or six years until 1531, when Giulio, who, unlike Raphael, never tolerated collaborators of any stature, got rid of him by having him sent to France in response to a request of Francis I's to Federigo Gonzaga for an artist of quality. Primaticcio was responsible for the Sala degli Stucchi, which is decorated with splendid friezes and ceiling lunettes of fine plaster reliefs. Giulio's other Mantuan works were decorations in the vast warren of the old Castello – the Reggia – where among other things, he painted a ceiling in the Sala di Troia. This room has a vaulted ceiling above a cornice, and Giulio here invented the perspective illusion of scenes taking place in an imaginary space above eye level. His incidents from the Siege of Troy are set on the cornice, and the centre of the ceiling is filled with clouds in which float zephyrs and other figures, while on the walls below the cornice are histories of Troy conceived in the more usual manner as flat pictures. This also was an idea with a future.

His other surviving architectural works are the house he built for himself and the internal façades of the tiltyard in the Reggia. His own house is best contrasted with Raphael's, for it is as wilful as the Roman one is serene. No order decorates the façade (*Pl. 20*): the windows follow in a quick sequence in the *piano nobile* (the fourth bay on the left of the door was added in 1800), each one with a triangular pediment jammed tightly within the relieving arch which has a heavily rusticated framework around it; below the string-course, which doubles as a window-sill, is a basement storey of more roughly rusticated blocks cut into by simple square windows below which is a real basement with small window

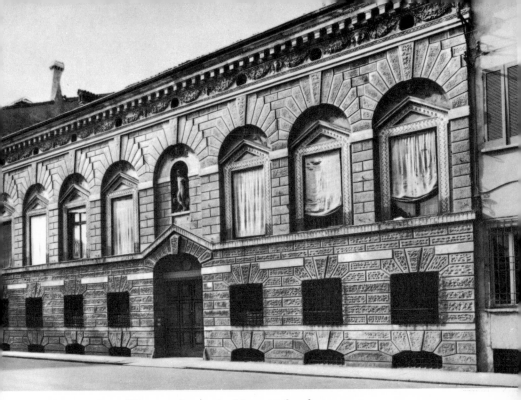

20 GIULIO ROMANO His own house in Mantua, façade, c. 1544

heads just peeping out of the ground as if they had slipped down into the earth. The door is quite plain, but the sharply pointed pediment above it is merely the string-course poked upwards while the architrave of the door also reappears threading its way along the basement between the rustications of the window frames. There is an entablature although there is no order to support it, and the rich garlands in the frieze are looped up over the tiny attic windows, while the bottom of the entablature rests directly on the projecting blocks of the keystones of the main window arches. Over the door is a niche conspicuously smaller than the windows, containing an Apollo, and in the head of every arch a mask caught like a nut in crackers between the pediment and the keystone. The result is controlled and disturbed, symmetrical yet perversely unbalanced. The tiltyard, or Cavallerizza, is a long courtyard divided evenly into bays, with a heavy rustication throughout,

39

21 PARMIGIANINO Ceiling of S. Maria della Steccata, Parma, 1531-9

wide arches below and heavy windows above, the bays divided by twisted, unevenly fluted columns derived ultimately from the twisted columns in Old St Peter's. The effect is colourful in the chiaroscuro sense, and of a fascinating perversity, since the column forms are at such variance with the fortified look of the rest of the wall. These emotional uses of the contrasts of plain and rough surfaces, of broad and flattened arches bearing heavy blocks simulating rough hewn stone, of simple Doric entablatures borne on the richest kind of decorative columns, creating effects of light and shadow, of movement, of confusion between forms proper to interiors and exteriors, and the sense of unease and astonishment caused to the knowledgeable spectator by the distortions of the classical canons, are the basic vocabulary of Mannerist architecture. It is essential that the spectator look at it with a discerning eye to recognize the violations, for in these surprises

40

lies the essence of the style. One of the fascinating things about Giulio is the isolation in which he worked after his move to Mantua; so far as it has been possible to discover, he never visited Florence, (for he travelled to Mantua via Loreto) or went further afield than Ferrara and Bologna, so that he could have known nothing by Michelangelo later than the *Moses*, nor could he have known much about Florentine developments, or Correggio in Parma. His only outside contacts, for that matter, were with Titian when he passed through Mantua on his way to Rome in 1545, when Vasari visited him in 1544, and when Cellini also visited him. Yet his perspective illusionism in the Palazzo del Tè, where figures stand upon the very edge of the frame and are painted in the most violent foreshortening, or float heavenwards so that they present chiefly the soles of their feet, are ideas current in Italy a decade or so later, and in particular in Parma at almost the same moment. But it is not so odd when one remembers that the great exemplar of illusionism in Mantua was Mantegna.

Although Parmigianino was born in Parma in 1503, and was commissioned to paint frescoes in Parma cathedral in 1522, and in S. Giovanni Evangelista in 1522-23, there is no evidence that he was ever directly Correggio's pupil. Certainly, he was strongly influenced by him, but late in 1523 he was in Rome, where the major influences on him became those of Raphael, whom he wanted to succeed, and Rosso, with whom he was closely associated. He also knew Perino del Vaga and Giulio Romano in Rome, so that he was in contact with all the painters at the heart of the Mannerist development. In 1527 he was working on the huge *Madonna and Child with St Jerome* (*Pl. 22*) during the Sack of Rome; this picture betrays his mixed artistic allegiances, the Madonna adapted from Raphael, yet with more than something of Michelangelo's heroic quality, the Baptist deriving distantly from Leonardo's celebrated gesture, and the St Jerome adapted from Correggio's figure of Daniel in the small frescoes under the arches in S. Giovanni Evangelista. The strongly modelled forms and lighting make the picture very Roman in feeling; one of the most telling characteristics is the enormous scale (over eleven feet high), and the rigorous 'Roman' draughtsmanship – no tender handling and soft light slipping over the forms and bathing them in Correggio's unearthly radiance, but a minute particularization with firm edges and a heavy chiaroscuro. Eventually he escaped from the horrors of the Sack of Rome, and after wandering about through Bologna, Verona, and Venice, he returned to Parma by 1530. There he was commissioned to paint frescoes in the church of S. Maria della Steccata (*Pl.* 21) but this work was fraught with difficulties between the patrons and the artist to such a point that they eventually sued him for the execution of the contract. They also tried to get Giulio Romano to take over part of the work, for which he did eventually provide drawings, but only with great misgiving because of his reluctance to interfere between another painter and his patrons.

Parmigianino's most famous work, beside the unfinished Steccata figures, is probably the Madonna known as the *Madonna del Collo Lungo* ('of the long neck') (*Pl. 38*), one of the key works in the development of Mannerist painting. The Virgin is in every way the Queen of Heaven, with strongly Raphaelesque features and long graceful hands; she sits enthroned, wrapped in a blue mantle draped carelessly over her white gown, and upon her lap the Christ Child lies sleeping, while angels crowd upon her from the side and watch with ecstatic expressions over the curiously elongated figure of the sleeping Child. Behind the Madonna is an enormous void, filled in the distance by the unfinished columns of a building, and at the base of the colonnade is a tiny gesticulating figure with a scroll. The violent dissonances of scale between the foreground and the background, the fantastically elongated proportions of the figures, the conscious disposition of limbs in poses of the most contrived gracefulness, all tend to create a feeling of exaggerated and sophisticated elegance. The *Madonna with St Zaccharias* (Uffizi), with the aged prophet in the foreground serving as a repoussoir, the melting St Catherine filling the same function in the Bologna *Madonna with Saints*, are further instance of his use of deliberately Raphaelesque types of the most *recherché* elegance in form and pose. Parmigia nino's great strength lay in this elegance and distinction and in his rigorously firm draughtsmanship; his weakness lay in his own temperament. Whether or not it was the horrors of the Sack that disturbed him, or his tormented neurosis was inherent, the result was the same; he died in tragic circumstances in 1540, and Vasari describes

22 PARMIGIANINO
*Madonna and Child
with St Jerome,* 1527

him as having changed from an elegant and delicate person into an unkempt and almost savage creature, obsessed with alchemy.

All Andrea del Sarto's pupils achieved eminence. Jacopo Pontormo, who was born in 1494, was first with Albertinelli, and possibly also with Piero di Cosimo, before coming – more as an assistant – into Sarto's workshop. His first works are strongly influenced by Fra Bartolommeo, and in 1516 his *Visitation* in the Annunziata court-yard shows the impact of his elders, with few hints, despite the way the subject is set into the picture space, and the woman and boy sit on the steps, of the turmoils to come. In 1518 he finished the *Madonna and Child with Saints* in S. Michele Visdomini in Florence. This picture is as epoch-making as Leonardo's *Last Supper*, in that it is a watershed for the emergence of the completely new stylistic development of Mannerism. It is a strange, almost convulsive work, blending uneasily forms derived from Leonardo and Raphael, with the Frate's ecstatic gestures and expressions, and the flickering patch-work of light and shadow superimposed on the negation of depth which first appears in Sarto. What this new attitude could lead to is clear from the *Joseph in Egypt* panel from a series painted to decorate a room between 1515-18 (*Pl. 23*). Here the thesis proposed by Man-nerism is fully elaborated: the painter is no longer to be bound by perspective, or by the necessity of presenting his subject in a rational, objective manner. He may use light and colour, chiaroscuro and proportion as he pleases; he may borrow from any source he chooses; the only obligation upon him is to create an interesting design, expressive of the ideas inherent in the subject, and the various parts need bear no relationship to each other. The colour must be evo-cative and beautiful in itself.

In 1521 he was commissioned to paint a large decoration in the Medici villa at Poggio a Caiano, in a scheme on which Sarto and Franciabigio were also employed. Eventually, Pontormo's part was limited to a lunette round a large circular window (*Pl. 24*); there is practically no internal cohesion between the marvellous figures in his fresco, which merely sit or lounge in almost abstract detach-ment under the drooping branches of a willow tree. The light is warm and glowing, the colour restrained and clear, the feeling gay and lighthearted, and the drawing of the nude man and the garland-

44

bearing urchins proves his close study of Michelangelo's *Battle* cartoon. Pontormo has a definite physical type, very tall with long legs and a compact head with a symmetrically oval face containing small features with huge wide-open eyes and a little half-open mouth – a face that is a screen upon which the emotions, chiefly of grief and anxiety, are reflected. He is at his greatest in his religious works, such as the frescoes of the *Passion* in the Certosa di Val d'Ema, near Florence, done between 1522-25. These are now no more than ghostly remains, and in comparison with his earlier (and later) works they can hardly be called Mannerist, for despite the occasional use of strongly *repoussoir* figures and an extreme expressiveness of face and gesture they are admirably clear, and their delicate and muted colour has little of the dramatic overtones of the S. Felicità *Deposition (Pl. 27)*. It is in these frescoes that he borrowed from Dürer, to the scandal of Vasari, who was quite blind to the scope which Dürer's engravings and woodcuts offered to artists seeking for new means of expression.

The very dark chapel in S. Felicità in Florence contains a superb *Annunciation* frescoed on the wall on either side of the win-

24 PONTORMO Lunette from Poggio a Caiano, *c.* 1

dow, symbolizing the Incarnation through which light came to the world, and upon the altar is a *Deposition* which continues the words of the Creed by representing the Sacrifice which the Mass celebrates. The colour of the *Deposition* takes into account the darkness of the chapel, so that it glows with an unearthly radiance of pinks, greenish

blues, pallid flesh tones, and a vivid orange scarlet. The forms of the dead Christ depend ultimately on Michelangelo's *Pietà* in St Peter's, but this work was now so well known that it is no evidence for Pontormo's having visited Rome; the influence of Michelangelo results partly from his having been in close contact with him in

25 Attributed to VASARI.
Drawing after Perino del Vaga.
Martyrdom of the Theban Legion

26 (*below*) PONTORMO
Martyrdom of the Theban Legion,
c. 1528/9

27 PONTORMO *Deposition, c.* 1528

28 PONTORMO *Halberdier, c.* 1527

Florence, and partly from the impact of Perino del Vaga's cartoon
for the *Martyrdom of the Theban Legion,* done in Florence in 1522-23
(*Pl. 25*). This work is filled with nudes in poses that demonstrate
the artist's ability to design figures interesting in themselves apart
from any meaning they may have in the context, and it caused great
excitement by introducing Roman ideas of Raphaelesque inspired
idealization, and antique decorative motives, while its subject stim-
ulated an interest in the dramatic possibilities of horror subjects.
It reinforced the ever-active impact of Michelangelo's *Battle* cartoon, by renewing the concentration on the heroic nude, which was
now to be joined to the new dramatic use of colour, which almost
superseded Sarto's imaginative chiaroscuro. Pontormo himself
painted a *Martyrdom of the Theban Legion,* which is almost an epitome
of all the characteristics of Mannerism in their most exaggerated
form, but it is possible that its date – about 1528-29 – may account
for much of his fascinated concentration on horror and violence
(*Pl. 26*). His last works were considered to be failures in his own

lifetime and are known only from his drawings; but he was among the really great draughtsmen of the sixteenth century. Pontormo was also a surprisingly fine portrait painter, perhaps because he endows his sitters with a vivid expressiveness and an air of neurotic sensibility. In his late years he became distinctly eccentric, and there were times when he lived the life of a recluse, refusing to see even Bronzino, who was practically an adopted son. He died in 1556.

Rosso and Pontormo virtually created Florentine Mannerism between them. Rosso was born in 1495, and his formative years are very obscure. Vasari was unable to assign him a master, commenting that he had ideas opposed to those who could have taught him, and he seems to have excelled Pontormo in individuality. He is clearly identifiable from about 1513 on, painting in a style which turns accepted Raphaelesque classicism upside down: compositions in the forms used by Fra Bartolommeo and Sarto, but without the construction of the one or the draughtsmanship and chiaroscuro of the other. Compared with Sarto's and Pontormo's performances in the

29 ROSSO *Madonna and Child with Saints*, 1518

30 MICHELANGELO *Pietà*. Drawing, *c.* 1519/20

Annunziata courtyard, Rosso's nearby *Assumption* of 1517 is a thin
and bloodless affair, with schematized versions of Pontormo's stylized facial types and the Frate's rhetorical gestures. His altarpiece
of the *Madonna and Child with Saints*, painted in 1518 for the Hospital of S. Maria Nuova (*Pl. 29*), filled the commissioners with
dismay when they saw it sketched in, for the saints looked to them
like devils; his first ideas must, then, have been considerably toned
down in execution, yet the results are often bizarre enough. The
skinny St Jerome, with limbs like a praying mantis, the distracted
Lear-like character glaring over the Child's shoulder lead on to
the ghostly apparitions in the altarpiece painted for the parish church
of Villamagna near Volterra, and prepare one for the very considerable shock of the *Descent from the Cross* in Volterra itself, painted
in 1521 (*Pl. 31*). In this work the main character is the colour, and
the colour is devoted to one end: a violent and emotional expressiveness which overrides everything else, and seeks only to provoke
in the spectator a thrill of horror and grief comparable with that

52

which shattered the men and women who helped to lift Christ from the Cross and bury Him. The drawing is not conceived as a means of describing forms, but as a means of stating ideas. The light is not a normal illumination nor even a poetic evocation: the scene is lit as if by lightning, and in the blinding flash the figures are frozen in their attitudes and even in their thoughts, while the great limp body of the dead Christ, livid green with reddish hair and beard, dangles perilously as His dead weight almost slips from the grasp of the men straining on the ladders. He too acknowledges, as the Pontormo *Deposition* does, Michelangelo's Roman *Pietà*, but the Christ of his *Deposition* is far more closely connected with a drawing for a *Pietà* which Michelangelo made about 1519-20, and which haunted Rosso to the end of his life (*Pl. 30*). His later *Pietà* painted in Rome, and now in Boston, is derived from it, and even the Paris one, despite its violently emotional colour, is a recension of the ideas of Michelangelo (with whom, incidentally, he was on very good terms). In 1523 Rosso went to Rome, and in 1527 was trapped there by the Sack, during which he is said to have undergone terrible sufferings. After the Sack he seems to have wandered restlessly around central Italy, ill, fearful of local hostility, involved in quarrels, yet dragging his large commissions after him from one resting place to another. Then he decided to go to France, passed through Venice on his way, and by the end of 1530 finally arrived at the French court, where he worked until the end of his life ten years later. Vasari, rather unkindly, said he committed suicide, but this must be wrong, since apparently he received a normal burial. Yet the nature of his art makes the statement plausible.

In Rome he was impelled by his admiration for Michelangelo to develop a grandiose treatment for the nude, which, seen through the Mannerism of his vision, produced such works as the extraordinary *Moses defending the daughters of Jethro* – a mass of huge bodies, jumbled in a violent struggle at the feet of a pallid semi-nude shepherdess surrounded by her frightened sheep (*Pl. 32*). The fantastic quality of his imagination, which emerged in his early drawing of the *Skeletons*, leads him to create pictures which never portray an event, but recreate its emotional impact. For Rosso, form has nothing to do with relief, and only peripherally with idealized nature: it is the means by which ideas are made visible.

The second generation in Florence consisted of Bronzino, Vasari, Salviati, as the chief painters, and Bandinelli, Cellini, Ammanati and Giovanni da Bologna as sculptors. Bronzino, born in 1503, was in Pontormo's studio from childhood, and from 1539 onwards was the chief court painter to the Medici ruler, Cosimo I, and his wife Eleanora of Toledo. For her he decorated the chapel in the Palazzo Vecchio, with frescoes of astonishing incoherence and fantastic colour, filled with the usual Mannerist conception of men in extreme foreshortenings and exaggerated musculature, and women of the most pallid and coldly classical beauty. The allegory painted in 1545, and destined to be sent to Francis I, *Venus, Cupid, Time and Folly*, is of a rebarbatively frigid eroticism (*Pl. 33*); in these years Bronzino also worked as a tapestry designer. Except for a visit to Rome between 1546-48, he was in Florence until his death in 1572, working as a court artist, with portraits bulking large in his *œuvre* (*Pl. 34*). They are exceptional in beauty and influence: cold, haughty faces, studied detachment, and aloof nobility seem to betray the watchful repression of emotion and the deadened sensibility resulting from life under a violent and capricious tyrant. From Cosimo's time onwards, art in Florence is mainly court art, for he believed in patronage as an appanage of power. He could not tempt Michelangelo back from Rome, but all the others he employed at times, and some constantly, interesting himself also in the establishment of Academies of Arts and Languages, drawing thus a veil of culture and learning over his harshly repressive police state. His long reign – 1537 to 1574 – covers virtually the full development of Mannerism, and its transition from the early stages of its revolt against classical perfection, with Pontormo and Rosso, to the final chilling inanities of the late decorations in the *studiolo* of the Palazzo Vecchio.

Vasari played the part of an impresario. He was born in 1511 and died in 1574; after being a pupil of Sarto and Bandinelli, he finally emerged as a passionate admirer of Michelangelo. He travelled round Italy, after the murder of his first patron, Alessandro de' Medici in 1537, painting wherever work was to be found, and it was during these years that the idea of the 'Lives' was born in him. In Rome he directed the building of the Villa Giulia for Julius III, did fresco decorations in the Cancelleria and the Vatican, and in Florence built the Uffizi (*Pl. 35*) – his major work – and painted fres-

33 BRONZINO *Venus, Cupid, Time and Folly*, 1545

32 ROSSO *Moses defending the daughters of Jethro, c.* 1523

34 BRONZINO
Ugolino Martelli, c. 1535

coes in the Palazzo Vecchio and in the dome of Florence Cathedral,
displaying the extent of his erudition and the limitations of his artistic
talent. His great monument is the 'Lives', first published in 1550, on
a severe scheme as an account of the arts of the past culminating
in the Life of Michelangelo – the only living artist to appear – and
a history of the fall and regeneration of the arts through the efforts
of Tuscans. The success of the book was enormous, and in 1568
he published a second, enlarged and revised, edition, containing the
lives of many other living artists. From the historical standpoint
this is all to the good, but it involved a corresponding weakening
of his original thesis. Vasari took his work as an historian very ser-
iously, and did his best to be accurate in his facts and attributions.
The 'Lives' has been much attacked for its errors, but without it the
history of the arts in Italy would be almost irrecoverable, and despite
his faults it must be remembered that he is four-hundred years nearer
the events than his critics. Michelangelo, who first thought poorly
of him, came to appreciate his ability and devotion, though after
the publication of the 1550 edition he virtually dictated a rival life

58

of himself which Condivi, his pupil, wrote up in 1553; but Michelangelo's view of his own career is as partisan in a different way as Vasari's, and his inaccuracies are deliberate.

Salviati is a more interesting painter than Vasari, whose close friend he was. He was in the Sarto workshop about 1529, and after the Siege, Vasari and he were together in Rome, where the influence of Raphael, and of sophisticated Raphael followers like Giulio Romano and Perino del Vaga, affected him deeply, as did Rosso. He also gathered ideas from his travels through north Italy, in Mantua, Venice and probably Parma, to judge from the impact of Parmigianino. He was always restless and peripatetic, with an elaborate decorative style, involved imagery, and fantastic perspective, managed in a consummate technique combining Michelangelesque drawing with the pale, brilliant colour general among Mannerist fresco painters. His splendid portraits and the *Triumphs* in Florence are probably his least Mannerist works, his frescoes in the Palazzo Sacchetti and the Farnese palace in Rome his most – and in fact the Farnese frescoes (his last major work before his death in

35 VASARI Screen from the Uffizi, built between 1560-74

1563) are among the most extravagant, amusingly witty, and sophisticated in all the genre (*Pl. 36*).

Possibly the most interesting of the non-Florentine Mannerist
painters was Beccafumi. Born in 1485/6, he belongs to the High
Renaissance generation, and his death in 1551 brought to an end
the long, and always emotionally directed, succession of great
Sienese painters. His years in Rome from 1510 to 1512 coincided
with the period of the Stanze and the Sistine Ceiling; yet soon after
his return to Siena in 1513 his work displayed characteristics nor-
mally associated with the Mannerism of the next decade. His later
use of lurid colour, extraordinary perspective and elaborate *contrapposto* probably reflect a knowledge of these stylistic elements
in central Italian painting, gained through the dispersal of artists
after the Sack (*Pl. 37*).

Of the sculptors, Bandinelli (1493-1560) was the least competent and most unfortunate, for he had to compete with the fiery and
uninhibited Cellini. His lumpish *Hercules and Cacus* of 1534 – described as a 'sack of walnuts' – displays its inadequacies only yards
away from Michelangelo's great *David*, which it was his avowed intention to surpass, and his major contribution to the arts was the part
he played in establishing Academies (his first was as early as 1531)
as art-schools, whereby eventually the workshop system of appren-

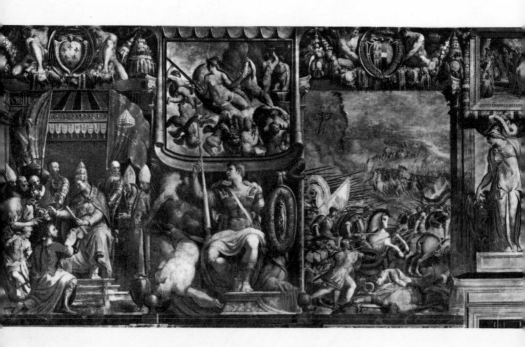

37 BECCAFUMI *Birth of the Virgin*

38 PARMIGIANINO *Madonna del Collo Lungo, c.* 1535

(*opposite*) SALVIATI *Triumph of anuccio Farnese*, after 1553

ticeship was superseded, not, perhaps, without as much being lost as was gained by the change.

Cellini is as famous a writer as he is a sculptor, for his 'Autobiography' is the raciest of all accounts of an artist's life, and also deeply revealing on the subservient relationships general between artists and their patrons. His reputation probably owes as much to his memoirs as it does to his art. He lived from 1500 to 1571, was trained as a goldsmith, went to Rome in 1519, and after his adventures during the Sack came back to Florence, and went on to France in 1537 to become one of the team of Italians working for Francis I. His *Nymph* (Louvre: of 1543-44) was once at Anet, and the celebrated salt-cellar in Vienna was begun in Rome and finished for Francis I. In 1545 he left France abruptly for reasons which he was perhaps wise not to have made very clear, and settled in Florence to become the great partisan of Michelangelo and the bane of Bandinelli's life. Fortunately he never attempted the aggrandisement of form or complication of pose adopted by the usual Michelangelo follower, but rather his synthesis of form and meaning. His masterpiece, the *Perseus* (*Pl. 40*) (1545-54) was commissioned for its present position in the Loggia dei Lanzi, and designed from the start to withstand the competition of Michelangelo's *David* and Donatello's *Judith*, and to put down Bandinelli's *Hercules*.

39 SALVIATI *Charity*, c. 1554/8

40 CELLINI *Perseus*, 1545-54

41 AMMANATI *Marine God* from the *Neptune Fountain*, 1563-75

Ammanati was born in 1511, and died in Florence in 1592. He was trained by Montorsoli, one of Michelangelo's assistants on the Medici Chapel, and also by Sansovino in Venice, and in Rome worked under the direct supervision of Michelangelo. His *Neptune Fountain (Pl. 41)* in Florence barely justifies this splendid background, and the most attractive parts of it are the bronze figures of nymphs and satyrs on the basin. It plays a large part in the history of the monumental fountain, for the mixture of the solidity of statuary and the evanescent patterns of light and moving water became a favourite sixteenth-century form. Ammanati also worked as an architect, designing the Ponte S. Trinita (1567-70) and the rusticated courtyard of the Pitti Palace (1558-70), as well as being involved in some aspects of the Villa Giulia in Rome.

The greatest sculptor in Florence after Michelangelo left was Giovanni da Bologna, a Fleming, born in 1529, who went to Italy to study about 1554. On his way home from Rome he stopped in Florence – and stayed there until he died in 1608. He is the creator

of types so distinctive that he is the epitome of all the ideas of grace
movement, classical beauty, strength and expression current in the
age of Mannerism. The *Rape of the Sabines* (*Pl. 42*), of 1582, in the
Loggia dei Lanzi, is the very type of the Mannerist group, with
multiple viewpoints and the maximum of movement and drama possible, and in his figures of Venus – mostly for fountains, but many
as small bronzes – Giambologna achieves the Mannerist ideal in
elongation and in conscious courtly elegance. His fountains are
masterpieces: the *Neptune Fountain* in Bologna, of 1563-7, was his
first, followed by a splendid series for various Medici villas and
gardens (*Pl. 43*), which includes the *Samson slaying the Philistine*
(begun about 1565, now in London, Victoria and Albert Museum).
With Michelangelo, he is a formative influence on the Baroque;
Bernini, for instance, though he reacted against the multiple viewpoint, remained strongly affected by the drama and expression of
Giambologna's works, and the development of fountain sculpture
became one of the great arts of Baroque.

42 GIAMBOLOGNA *Rape of the Sabines*, 1582   43 GIAMBOLOGNA *Venus*, c. 1572/3

44 PERUZZI Sala delle Prospettive, Villa Farnesina, *c.* 1515

If one removes from an account of sixteenth-century art in Rome Raphael and his studio and all Michelangelo's works, then little is left. Only Sebastiano del Piombo remains as a major resident painter, and not just a visitor, like Vasari, Ammanati and Salviati, with the architects Peruzzi, Vignola, Giacomo della Porta and Domenico Fontana.

Baldassare Peruzzi was born about 1481 and began as a painter in Siena. He came to Rome about 1503, and died there in 1536. He went into the Bramante shop, and produced a plan for St Peter's which is a variation, though simplified, of Bramante's centrally planned project. He also built two palaces in Rome: the Villa Farnesina between 1509-11, and the Palazzo Massimi alle Colonne, which is his last work. The Farnesina was built for the banker Agostino Chigi, a Sienese for whom Raphael decorated the Farnesina with the *Galatea* and supervised Giulio Romano's Loggia decorations of the story of Psyche. The Farnesina was planned much on the lines of a *villa suburbana* – not as a place of residence, but a

66

45 PERUZZI Sala delle Prospettive, detail of painted colonnad

pavilion at which to spend the hot summer days. It consists of a
central block with two wings projecting on the garden front, and
between them an open loggia (now glazed in), where the painted
decorations are. Originally the outside walls were also frescoed, but
now the only part of the exterior decoration is the richly ornamental
frieze. Upstairs, in the *gran salone*, Peruzzi painted one of the early
Roman illusionistic decorations. At first sight, it appears as if the
room opens on to a loggia, through the columns of which there is
a view of Rome; in fact, all is illusion, and loggia, columns, and
statues in niches, are all painted (*Pls. 44, 45*). After the death of
Raphael in 1520, Peruzzi became joint head of the works at St
Peter's, but he could do little, and after the Sack, during which he
suffered great hardship, he escaped to Siena. He was re-appointed
to the works at St Peter's in 1530, but did not return to the city
permanently until 1535, and he died there in the following January.
During these last years he designed the Palazzo Massimi alle

46 PERUZZI Façade of the Palazzo
Massimi alle Colonne, Rome, *c.* 1535

Colonne, for a family of brothers who shared the site, but required
separate houses. The façade is the first to accept the requirements
of the site to the extent of curving with the street corner on which
the palace stands, and the forms display strange dissonances which
have caused it to be called the first truly Mannerist building, though
in fact it was built long after the Palazzo del Tè. The columns
of the portico are spaced irregularly, and are coupled and then
single with a closing pilaster, with an equally odd rhythm in the
windows above, and these again are surmounted by small mezzanine and attic windows with the flat leatherwork patterns of northern Mannerism around them, and are almost without projection
in a rusticated wall surface. The courtyard has the staircase offset,
to rise into a large, elaborate loggia, and the curious disposition
of the front windows is reflected here by the strange openings below
the loggia, which look like windows, but are, in fact, designed to
give extra light to the entrance loggia behind the columns, but they
so confuse the delimitation of the storeys that they effectively

disguise the disproportion between the ground and the first floors
(*Pl. 46*).

Sebastiano del Piombo, who came from Venice to work on the
decoration of the Farnesina, found himself part of the Raphael
circle. He did some decorative frescoes there, but his portraits during these years are his finest works. He manages to combine the
feeling and psychological interest of Giorgione's portraits with
Raphael's largeness of manner: the so-called *Dorothea* in Berlin (*Pl.
48*), or the portrait of *Cardinal Carondelet with his Secretary* (*Pl. 47*),
with the typically Venetian still-life interest in the foreground, and
the splendidly Roman colonnade behind, show his development of a
blend of Venetian and Roman characteristics. It is also obvious that
Sebastiano's rich Venetian colour influenced Raphael somewhat,
particularly in the Stanza dell'Eliodoro, and he was to have an effect on Michelangelo as well. Round about 1516, Sebastiano trans-
ferred his admiration from Raphael to Michelangelo, to the point
that he described Raphael and his assistants as 'quel sinagogo' –
'that clan'. The new influence is clear in works like the Viterbo
Lamentation and the *Flagellation* in S. Pietro in Montorio, which is
reputedly based on a Michelangelo drawing. Certainly, Michelangelo
did provide him with drawings for his compositions, notably for

SEBASTIANO *Cardinal Carondelet, c.* 1512   48 SEBASTIANO *Dorothea, c.* 1512

49 SEBASTIANO
Raising of Lazarus, 1517-19

the *Pietà* now at Úbeda in Spain. The rivalry with Raphael was accentuated by the commission for the *Raising of Lazarus (Pl. 49)* (1517-19), painted in competition with the *Transfiguration*, but it is not in vast machines of this order that his virtues are obvious, so much as in simpler dramatic subjects like the stark Viterbo *Lamentation* or the rich colour and sober form of small devotional works like the *Madonna and Child with a Donor*, in London. While his portraits continue to be superb (*Pl. 50*), his conscious attempts at grandiose feeling become empty and even vapid. In 1531 he took minor orders on receiving a papal sinecure of the Seal, hence the Roman name of Sebastiano 'del Piombo'. Vasari records that he became very lazy with the passage of time, and immoderately addicted to the pleasures of the table. He died in 1547. His slight influence on Michelangelo was in the direction of enriching the colour of some

70

of the figures in the *Ancestors of Christ* in the Sistine ceiling; here and there one of them shows a more Venetian painterly feeling and a looser technique.

Of the other architects, Fontana was principally an engineer who, in conjunction with Sixtus V during his short papacy from 1585-90, replanned Rome as a modern city, laying out the new roads which are still its main arteries, and bringing in new aqueducts to supply the great fountains of the Aqua Felice and the Trevi. Giacomo della Porta became official Architect to the Roman People, and had a hand in every large project in Rome until his death in 1602, but little he built is memorable on its own account. With Fontana, he erected Michelangelo's dome of St Peter's, which they altered somewhat in the process, and he also completed the Campidoglio, where he altered Michelangelo's design for the central window of the Conservatori, the exit roads and the pavement pattern. He finished Vignola's Gesù, where he spoilt the façade by changing the design altogether.

50 SEBASTIANO
Cardinal Pole, c. 1537

The great architect in Rome after Michelangelo was Vignola. He was born near Modena in 1507, and he began by drawing classical antiquities in Rome in the mid-1530s, and in 1541-43 he spent eighteen months in Fontainebleau with Primaticcio. He first appears as an architect at the Villa Giulia (*Pls. 51-53*) built for Pope Julius III from 1550 onwards, working in association with Vasari, who seems to have been the *entrepreneur* for this commission, and Ammanati who did the sculpture and the garden design. The main block of the villa has a strongly rusticated entrance porch in a flat façade, five bays wide, with heavy keystones and rusticated coigns below, with a simpler, flatter, more decorative treatment in the upper storey. From the garden side the contrast is complete, for to the uncompromising rectangles of the front corresponds a wide, sweeping semi-circular loggia with colonnaded openings on either side of a triumphal arch entrance, the barrel vaults of the loggia being painted with a charming decoration of vine arbours. The long garden is enclosed by a decorative wall pierced by a door; once through this another complete surprise meets the eye, for the garden here is sunken, and descends by semi-circular staircases to a deep nymphaeum (*Pl. 52*), where the water-lilies grow in the fountain that continues into a grotto, and behind, at the top of more staircases is a simple garden ending in a little temple. The whole charm of the place is in its evocation of coolness, of dripping rocks and statues sprayed by jets of water, of an escape from the sun and the public side of papal life to privacy and relaxation.

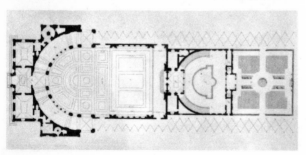

51 VIGNOLA
Plan and section of the Villa Giulia, Rome, 1550

52 VIGNOLA Nymphaeum of the Villa Giulia

53 VIGNOLA Garden front of the Villa Giulia

54 VIGNOLA Villa Farnese, Caprarola, after 1559

55 Section of the Villa Farnese, Caprarola

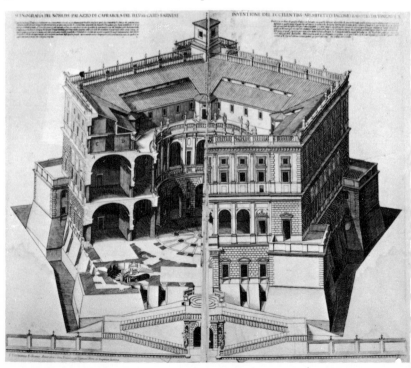

56 VIGNOLA Spiral staircase in the Villa Farnese, Caprarola

57 VIGNOLA Courtyard of the Villa Farnese, Caprarola

The villa at Caprarola was not the same kind of retreat. It was the centre of the Farnese estates, and was begun originally about 1521 by Antonio da San Gallo the Younger and Peruzzi as a fortified pentagon, but remained no more than foundation and a basement until Vignola began work there in 1559 (*Pls. 54-57*). The house – which served rather the same purpose as the 'prodigy' houses of the newly-landed English gentry seeking to mask the newness of their wealth and power – contained suites for summer and winter residence, built around a circular courtyard with arcades up and down, and a very flat barrel vault to the lower arcade. Inside, a circular stair rises, like the winding stair Bramante built in the Vatican Belvedere, to the *gran salone*. The most striking feature of Vignola's architecture is its careful avoidance of any of the more obvious Mannerist tricks, such as those in the Palazzo del Te. What he essays is, in some ways, a return to Bramante's simplicity and order, and an escape from the visual confusions and richness of ornament of Michelangelo. His detailing is flat, his rustication shallow, his arches plain, his order kept deliberately to Doric and Ionic, and

58 VIGNOLA Engraving of design for the façade of the Gesù, 1570

59 VIGNOLA Plan of the Gesù, Rome, 1568

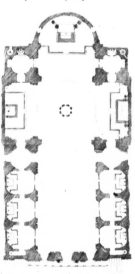

60 VIGNOLA S. Andrea in Via Flaminia, Rome, 1554

while the famous staircase is very decorative, there is no change in
the order as there was in Bramante's, but only a restrained Doric
throughout. Vignola, in fact, achieves the surprising feat of converting Bramante into another kind of classical model, like antiquity.

His churches were equally influential. The Gesù – the mother-
church of the Jesuit Order – was begun in 1568 on a very strict
brief prepared by his patron, Cardinal Farnese, which laid down the
importance of the preacher being audible in all parts (*Pls. 58, 59*).
This limited the building to a wide, barrel-vaulted nave, for acous-
tic reasons, and Vignola's solution was a return to the plan of Alberti's S. Andrea in Mantua of 1470, in that he adopted the aisleless
form with deep side chapels, leading to a wide crossing with an
apse behind the main altar. The site made this necessary also, and
only clerestorey windows light the nave, which in turn means that

77

the domed crossing is in a blaze of light. Vignola's original designs called for restraint, bareness even, in the interior decoration, but during the seventeenth century the church received one of the most exuberant Baroque decorations, so that the interior no longer corresponds to the architect's ideas. Neither does the façade, for Vignola died in 1573 when the church was only at cornice level. Giacomo della Porta finished it, adding his own façade, which is far from being as interesting or sensitively worked out as the original design. The Gesù, as the chief church of the most militant religious Order, was extremely influential, since most Jesuit churches followed it everywhere the Order penetrated.

During the work on the Villa Giulia Vignola built a tiny church, S. Andrea in Via Flaminia, close by. This he designed as a rectangle, with an oval dome over it, though from the outside the novelty of the shape is not immediately apparent (*Pl. 60*). In his small church, S. Anna dei Palafrenieri designed at the end of his life for the papal grooms and built chiefly by his son, he transfers the idea of an oval dome to the ground plan, giving the church an axis on the length of the oval by the position and depth of the entrance and the main altar. The walls of the chapel are articulated by large columns, and from these rise the ribs of the dome. From these simple beginnings came the interest in circular and oval plans during the Baroque period, for Bernini's S. Andrea al Quirinale and Borromini's S. Carlino are elaborations of an idea which started with Vignola. It is, however, important that all these small centrally planned churches were primarily private chapels, not grand or parish churches designed for large congregations. For these, Vignola's Gesù remained the preferred model. Vignola's remaining work of lasting importance was his great illustrated treatise, 'Regola delli Cinque Ordini d'Architettura', published in 1562. It is far more scholarly than Serlio and, with Palladio's 'Quattro Libri' of 1570, established the type of the learned yet informative work which lies at the base of academic example and precept. It became the textbook of all aspiring architects, and also of their patrons, and its countless editions spread the academic view of antiquity and of Bramante and Renaissance architecture far and wide over Europe.

CHAPTER THREE

Venice

For virtually ten years after the Sack of Rome in 1527 there was no money or scope for patronage in either Rome or Florence. Venice escaped the worst of the wars and invasions, and became a place of refuge chiefly for architects, since the great differences between Venetian and central Italian painting made it difficult for painters from outside to compete with the native product. In architecture, things were rather different, in that Venice was still a Gothic city, overshadowed by a great Byzantine past. Long after classical forms had become the norm in Florence, the Ca' d'Oro, built between 1427-36 as a masterpiece of Venetian Gothic, was far from being the last example of palaces in similar style. The form of Venetian palaces is different from Florentine, in that land in Venice is very precious, and few but the very grandest houses could have internal courtyards. The chain of palaces on the Grand Canal tended to turn the city into a sequence of façades, so that the architecture developed a definitely scenographic quality. The normal form of Venetian palace has the ground – or water-level – floor reserved to kitchens and other offices, and on the first floor a great living-room in the middle of the building looks out on to the fascinating pageant of everyday life on the city's main thoroughfare. The first introduction of new forms came as late as the 1480s, but hardly consisted of more than the systematization of the façade on a central axis, with the *gran salone* in the middle over the entrance, the staircase relegated to the back of the house, and the grouping of the principal windows in an ordered bay sequence. This type of ordered façade still co-existed with a modified Gothic window form, and even as late as the Palazzo Vendramin-Calergi, by Mauro Codussi, finished in 1509, the two-light arched top window, enclosed in a round-headed arch with a roundel in the centre, is the accompaniment to a central

61 SANMICHELI Palazzo Bevilacqua, Verona, *c.* 1530

Italian use of a classical order, even if this is treated with a good deal of latitude in the arrangement of coupled and single columns on the same façade.

After the Sack, Sanmicheli and Sansovino came to Venice and both became architects to the State. Serlio also came, and published the first parts of his treatise in Venice, but he left for France in 1540, and does not appear to have been much employed. Michele Sanmicheli was a Veronese, born in 1484, who went to Rome when he was sixteen and trained in the workshop of Antonio da Sangallo. He was in Orvieto from 1509, and worked in that district for nearly twenty years before returning to his native Verona, which belonged to Venice. He worked mainly on fortifications, not only in the

80

63 SANMICHELI Porta Palio, Ver

62 SANMICHELI
Palazzo Grimani, Venice,
begun in 1550s

64 SANSOVINO The Mint, Venice, begun *c.* 1537

Veneto, but in Venetian territories overseas – Corfu, Dalmatia, Crete – that had to be defended against the Turk. His buildings are therefore few; mostly palaces in Verona (*Pl. 61*) and Venice (*Pl. 62*), some fine gateways, and the Cappella Pellegrini attached to the church of S. Bernardino in Verona. His city gates present a strongly rusticated, and defensive side to an aggressor, and are closely based on the forms of Roman gates, and on the courtyard façades of the Palazzo del Tè (*Pl. 63*). In his palace designs he ranges from simple variations on Raphael's house, made more decorative by sculpture round the windows, to very elaborate structures, richly decorated, with extra floors contrived by inserting mezzanines and attics within the main divisions marked out by the orders articulating

65 SANSOVINO Library and Loggetta, Venice, begun 153

the façades. The Cappella Pellegrini is a centrally planned chapel with a coffered dome, based ultimately on the Pantheon, but here again the Roman device of the twisted fluting, which he knew from a Roman gate in Verona, Porta dei Borsari, is a legitimate borrowing from a classical source. He died in Verona in 1559.

Jacopo Sansovino was born in Florence in 1486 and died in Venice in 1570. He began as a sculptor under Andrea Sansovino, whose name he adopted, and he continued working as a sculptor even after he settled in Venice and became the chief architect to the city. He was in Giuliano da San Gallo's workshop in Rome in 1505-6, and thus in the Bramante circle, and first began building in 1518. He was appointed City architect in Venice in 1529, and worked there to the end of his long life, his greatest buildings being the Library, the Mint, and the Loggia at the base of the Campanile; he also made the great courtyard staircase at the Doge's palace and the two statues at the top, and built several of the most splendid palaces on the Grand Canal (*Pl. 66*).

The long façade of the Library is deliberately rich and decorative. It was a public commission intended for splendour of effect; it faced the Doge's Palace across the Piazzetta, and had a similar arcade system on the ground floor, echoing the Procuratie buildings on the far side of the Piazza di S. Marco, and made a contin-

uous open loggia for the little shops which have always been a feature of the square. Sansovino used the form of the double arcade, Doric below and Ionic above, like a Roman courtyard, with the window arches in the upper storey richly ornamented with sculpture on the keystones and in the spandrels, and a superbly rich frieze with swags and *putti* under the cornice, the whole crowned by a balustrade with obelisks and statues to make a decorative line against the sky. The Mint, next door, had a rusticated order, totally different proportions, much squatter (the top storey is a later addition), and intentionally defensive in appearance as well as fireproof inside, with only vaulted rooms and no wood in the construction. The object was to make the Venetian gold coinage visually stable as well as safe. The little Loggia of the Campanile is really an even richer continuation of the Library. All these façades tell as sequences of voids spaced out by richly decorative columns and arches, and form a superb foil to the arcade system of the Doge's Palace and St Mark's on the other side of the square. Add to these architectural effects the pale pink and cream of the pattern of the stonework of the Doge's Palace, the warm russet brick of the Campanile, the mosaics of the basilica, the green copper domes, the dazzling light and the dancing reflections off the water, and the result is a deliberate scene-setting designed to achieve magnificence of effect, and also a colourful pictorial quality, completely unarchitectural in the Roman and Florentine sense, but admirably suited to the site and to the character of Venetian art (*Pls. 64, 65*).

The Library was begun in 1537, and was not finished until after Sansovino's death. But Sansovino's architecture had a major effect on Venetian art; he introduced the new forms of Florentine and Roman Renaissance buildings into Venice, even though he made them richer and more decorative than they ever were in their original habitat, and this influenced Venetian painting towards an even greater opulence of effect. The architecture of Veronese's religious and secular decorations is inspired by Sansovino: the splendid loggias in the vast banqueting scenes that pass as the *Marriage at Cana*, or *Christ in the House of Levi*, or that form the background to the *Darius* in the National Gallery, London, are derived from these superbly decorative buildings, which the painter modified always in the direction of greater richness. Titian was only rarely

84

66 SANSOVINO Palazzo Corner della Ca' Grande, begun 1537

interested in painted architecture; few of his scenes, except the *Presentation*, have anything more than the sketchiest indications of an architectural setting. Tintoretto's architecture is much more fantastic than anything Sansovino ever built, and he borrows largely from Serlio for many of his very curious constructions.

Andrea Palladio, too, acknowledged his debt to Sansovino by designing the Basilica in Vicenza as a modified version of the Library. He was born in 1508 and died in 1580, and spent most of his life in Vicenza, where he designed a number of splendid palaces, and the celebrated villas in the neighbourhood which exercized so great an influence on English eighteenth-century architecture. He also built churches in Venice, and one of them – S. Giorgio Maggiore, on the marvellous island site across the lagoon facing St

85

67 PALLADIO Palazzo Chiericati, Vicenza, begun in 1550s

Mark's – is worthy to rank among the world's most beautiful churches. The Basilica (*Pl. 68*), which was not a church, but a recasing of a medieval hall in order to restore and enlarge it, is in two storeys like the Library, and introduces at the beginning of his career in 1549 the so-called Palladian motive (which is classical by origin) of a triple opening consisting of a central arch borne on columns, flanked by a rectangular opening on either side, similar to the window arrangement in the Library. Palladio's Basilica also stresses the verticals more than Sansovino does, and the total effect is one of an alternation of strong members framing large voids to create a bold sequence of light and dark. His palaces in Vicenza (*Pl. 67*) acknowledge distantly the forms evolved in Raphael's

86

68 PALLADIO Basilica, Vicenza, 1549 onwar‹

House, and in Giulio Romano's House in Mantua, but vary their systems of a basement supporting a colonnaded façade with great skill and inventiveness. All Palladio's palaces are built of brick, faced with stucco; most have a plan symmetrical about a central axis, and often the rooms inside are also planned to repeat about the axis of the courtyard; they all combine convenience with an air of discreet opulence. His villas pursue these aims even further, for they combine the usefulness of a working farm in the midst of a family estate, with the convenience and delight of a country villa lived in during the oppressive heat of the summer months. They are inspired by the classical *villa rustica* type of country house, and are quite different in purpose from the classical *villa suburbana* of which Raphael's Villa Madama, or Giulio's Palazzo del Tè, are grandiose examples. The Villa Rotonda, of 1550, built on a slight eminence as a cubic block with symmetrically planned rooms round a central domed circular hall, with four identical colonnaded porticoes with wide flights of steps, one on each of its four fronts, is justly his most famous building (*Pl. 73*); but the Villa Maser, much smaller and more intimate, with its interior decorated by

69 PALLADIO
S. Giorgio Maggiore,
Venice, façade, 1566

Veronese with superb frescoes (*Pls. 74, 75*), or the Villa Malcontenta, where the steps flow down on either side from the grand colonnaded portico towards the calm waters of the Brenta Canal in which it stands reflected, are creations as full of genius as they are of variety and charm. Some of these very grand villa designs remained merely as designs, published in 1570 in his treatise, 'Quattro Libri dell'Architettura' – one of the most influential of all architectural treatises, and the foundation of English Palladianism – and in them the central villa block extends on either side in wings attached by quadrant arcades, to combine comfort and grandeur with economy and utility, as he himself described them (*Pl. 71*).

Palladio's Venetian churches are of great splendour. Both S. Giorgio Maggiore (1566) (*Pls. 69, 70*) and the Redentore (1576) were designed for the ceremonial visits paid yearly by the Doge, but whereas the Redentore is restrained and modest in decoration, as befits a Franciscan church, S. Giorgio, a wealthy Benedictine

88

70 PALLADIO S. Giorgio Maggiore, Venice, interior

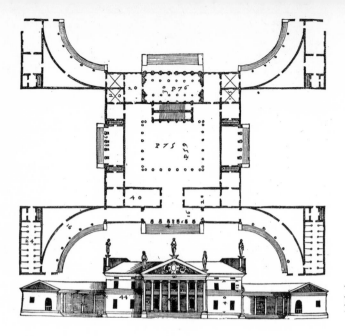

71 PALLADIO
Plan of
Villa Mocenigo

72 PALLADIO Palazzo Porto Colleoni, Vicenza. Drawing

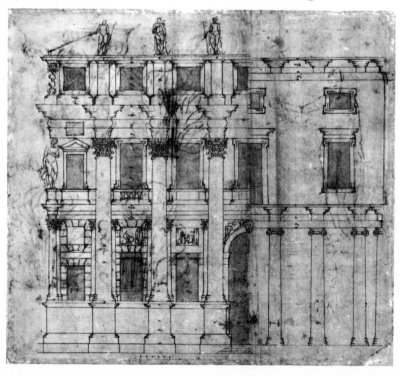

73 PALLADIO Villa Rotonda, begun 1550

house, is of great richness, built of pale Istrian stone, with a red and white chequerboard marble floor and white marble statues in niches in the aisles, giving an effect of cool magnificence. The façades of both churches are totally new in design. Instead of the usual two-storey front, with a pedimented upper part joined by volutes to the wider lower part extended on either side to front the aisles – the commonest type of Counter-Reformation and Baroque type derived ultimately from Alberti's Early Renaissance design at S. Maria Novella in Florence – Palladio creates a façade of two storeys, by impacting two classical temple fronts one upon the other, a tall one for the central part, and a wider, squatter one extending over the side aisles; and he unites them by continuing the details of one to become part of the main members of the other. This novel form he first tried out in the façade of S. Francesco della Vigna in Venice, where he was employed to make a new front for an existing church. Both S. Giorgio and the Redentore have large

74 VERONESE Frescoes in the Villa Maser, begun *c.* 1560

domed, apsidal east ends, with screens separating the monastic choir
from the high altar, and large transepts with apsidal ends and semi-
domes. Both were used for the impressive choral music written
for St Mark's, which required the use of separate choirs to create
the full polyphonic effect, but S. Giorgio, as much the larger church,
also had space for altars in wide aisles (the Redentore is aisle-less),
most of them containing splendid altarpieces, and for a pair of
pictures in the choir flanking the high altar, painted by Tintoretto
– *The Gathering of the Manna* and the *Last Supper*, his last important
works.

Paolo Veronese was, as his name indicates, born in Verona, about
1528. A typical man of his age, he reflects a large number of influences – Titian, Michelangelo, Giulio Romano, Parmigianino all

75 VERONESE Frescoes in the Villa Maser

76 VERONESE *Triumph of Venice, c.* 1585

contribute something to the extrovert and splendidly decorative qualities of his art. Rarely does Veronese stir one either by his insight, or by any emotion or tenderness; he amazes, exhilarates by his energy and brilliance, by his colour, the number of figures knitted into a composition, by the daring and complexity of his feats of illusionism and perspective.

His first works show mainly the influence of Titian's Pesaro altarpiece, in their use of the asymmetrical setting of the figures with huge columns and high pedestals, but after he arrived in Venice, about 1553, where he worked continuously until his death in 1588, he began the illusionistic ceilings for S. Sebastiano, with the story of Esther, a form he continued first in his dazzling frescoes for the Villa Maser, built by Palladio, and then in the Doge's Palace. The Villa Maser frescoes (*Pls. 74, 75*) probably follow a visit to Rome in 1560, and they are important, not only for their sheer delight and their suitability to their beautiful setting, but also because they introduce pure landscape panels, as a genre on its own, thus paralleling ideas which were being developed in Fontainebleau. The Doge's Palace frescoes came mostly after the 1577 fire, and include the magnificent *Triumph of Venice* (*Pl. 76*) in the Sala del Maggior Consiglio of about 1585, an example of illusionism which presages the most fantastic produced by Roman Baroque painters a half century later. In 1573 he found himself in trouble with the Inquisition, accused of indecorum through his introduction of figures of German mercenaries, buffoons, dogs, and such-like light relief into his huge pictures in which a scene of secular feasting has a religious motive concealed somewhere in the crowds. His defence – that the artist is free to fill his canvas as he pleases, and cannot be blamed for disposing a large crowd of supernumerary extras on his stage – is the classic defence of the artist against the limitations which a philistine might seek to impose on his vision. The Inquisitor, in this case, had the last word, since Veronese did in fact

77 VERONESE *Feast in the House of Levi*, 1573

rename his picture the *Feast in the House of Levi* (*Pl. 77*). Some of his smaller religious works, such as the *Baptist preaching* of the mid 1560s (*Pl. 78*), combine an almost Mannerist viewpoint with astonishing colour and unusual composition, and many of his mythologies are of a memorable eroticism, which often manages to be amusing as well. His large family pieces – the Cuccina family, presented to the Virgin in a *Madonna and Child* of about 1571, now in Dresden, or the Pisani family in the *Family of Darius before Alexander* of about 1565-70, in London, are extensions of the normal re-religious picture with donors, which have the result of confusing the borderline between the religious and the secular, since the portrait aspect often takes precedence over the content. This kind of licence is surprising in a painter who was known for his strict religious observance, and for the probity of his morals. His most striking figures are certainly his opulent, golden-haired Venetian women, trailing their brocades behind them like slow-moving, majestic, jewel-studded galleons drifting across the lagoons. With these splendid creatures, half vision, half real, rank his true portraits, which, though few, make an interesting contrast with Titian's. They concentrate perhaps less on the character of the sitter than on his – or her, for some of his finest are of women as magnificent as any of his saints or Venuses – social position, and in this he followed rather than led along the path Paris Bordone had marked out.

Of the lesser men, Bordone (1500-71) came from Treviso, and from his training and life in Venice followed in the wake of Titian, except that he developed into a portrait painter in a style which blended Titian's colour and ease, with something of the Florentine court painter's frigidity and concentration on the social presence of his sitter (*Pl. 79*). He was in great demand as a portraitist, visited France in 1538, and was in Augsburg in 1540, where his Venetian richness influenced the German court painters such as Amberger and Pencz probably as much as did Titian, in that the externals of his style were more easily imitated than Titian's deeper qualities of perception. Bonifazio de' Pitati was a man of Titian's, rather than Veronese's generation, being born in 1487, and he was a pupil of Palma Vecchio. He ran a large workshop in Venice, and imitated Titian and Giorgione, though aspects of his art range very widely indeed, and Lotto and Bordone are reflected in him as well. He died

96

VERONESE *The Baptist preaching, c.* 1565

79 BORDONE
Portrait of a Man

in 1553. Andrea Schiavone, a Dalmatian from Zara, who died in
Venice in 1563, must have been working from the late 1520s. He is
recorded as self-taught, mostly by imitating Giorgione and Titian,
and also the engravings of Parmigianino, and possibly Correggio as
well. Certainly, he imports into Venice a strangely ecstatic quality,
absent as a rule from Venetian art, and his shot colour schemes
and violent effects of *contrapposto*, support the argument that central Italian Mannerism was important in his development. It is from
Schiavone's studio that Tintoretto probably came, despite his claim
in later years to have been a pupil of Titian.

The other important painter contemporary with Tintoretto was
Bassano. This was the name of a family of painters called da Ponte,
who came from Bassano in the mountains above Venice. The father,
Francesco, was a modest follower of the Bellini; his son Jacopo,
born between 1510-18, lived and worked most of his life in Bassano,

where he died in 1592. He was the genius of the family, developing a bold, energetic style out of his training with Bonifazio de' Pitati and the influence of Titian. He evolved a new kind of subject – the rustic genre scene, with animals and herdsmen, peasants and farm servants, set in mountainous and stormy landscapes, and his religious pictures also exploit the same vein, with flocks of sheep and cattle accompanying the adoring shepherds to the manger (*Pl. 80*). His dark and lowering landscapes, the profusion of his still-life details, the dramatic nature of his lighting effects, his sharp perspective, are features that sometimes follow, but sometimes accompany, Tintoretto's similar experiments. His sons Francesco, who committed suicide in the year of his father's death, and Leandro, who lived until 1622, worked in the Venetian end of the family business, and continued their father's style, with stronger influence from Tintoretto. Leandro also painted very fine dark portraits, in a style dependent on Tintoretto's.

With Tintoretto the Renaissance in Venice comes to an end. He was born in Venice in 1518, and very little is known of his early years, except that he claimed to have been in Titian's studio – from which tradition has it that he was expelled for caricaturing the

master – and possibly worked with Schiavone and Paris Bordone. No work can be ascribed to him before 1545, although he figures in the records as an independent painter by 1539. What he aimed at was clear enough. He sought to combine Titian's colour with Michelangelo's drawing, and in this thoroughly Mannerist design he was completely successful, because, in fact, though he borrowed from both, he derived from neither. He knew the principal works by Michelangelo and Raphael through engravings and casts; he could have known them in no other way, since he is not recorded as ever having left Venice, but by now the traffic in engravings was such that very little of note was not generally known throughout Italy, and in northern Europe. He must also have owned small models of Michelangelo's Medici Chapel figures, since drawings exist of the recumbent tomb figures in positions which could not have been drawn otherwise. From the first he develops a counterpoint of swaying figures, composing his pictures in friezes; the figures are aligned in a series of sharp and almost unrelated verticals, broken only by a few broad gestures. The figures, in, for instance, the *St Ursula and her Virgins* of about 1545, swing in a long, slow zigzag from one side of the picture to the other right back into the far depths, the front plane being filled in the arched top by the swift plunging flight of the angel. The magnificent *Esther* at Hampton Court, also of about 1545, is a perfect example of another Mannerist device: the momentary movement caught and held. Everything is in motion; the king rises, Esther slips fainting towards the ground, her women move to catch her, the crowd strains forward to see, and the instant the artist has recorded is as transitory as the passage of time itself.

In 1548 he made his reputation with the *Miracle of St Mark rescuing a Slave (Pl. 81)*; in point of time, it is contemporary with the beginning of Veronese's career, and with Titian's maturity. It was for him what the *Assumption* had been for Titian, and before beginning it Tintoretto had subjected himself to a patient training in Florentine draughtsmanship, largely to modify the kind of loose Mannerism which he had enjoyed until now, and which Bonifazio de' Pitati specialized in. The composition of the *Miracle of St Mark* is very carefully worked out; each figure is balanced by another, each motive matched by a counterpart, and though the picture is a very large and crowded one, even the most subordinate figures are fitted

81 TINTORETTO *Miracle of St Mark rescuing a Slave*, 1548

in with scrupulous care. The St Mark plunging to save the captive who had called upon him in his extremity is a daring figure in the most unusual foreshortening, and the colour – strong, singing, unexpected in its contrasts and harmonies – is sudden, brilliant and astonishing. This is the first picture in which Tintoretto displays all that he had learned from Titian, and makes full use of the start which Titian gave him stylistically, but, true to his own vision, he concentrates his forces into a single fleeting moment, and carries it all through in one surging movement and rhythm. Michelangelo makes a brief appearance in the figures over the distant door, and the plummetting St Mark could derive equally from the Sistine Ceiling, or Raphael's Loggie decorations.

82 TINTORETTO *Presentation of the Virgin*, 1551-2

But the Mannerist elements could not long remain dormant. In the *Presentation of the Virgin* of 1551-52 (*Pl. 82*) the space is irrational, the steps essential to the iconography are used as much to break up the flow of the composition as to hold it together, and the perspective is used to increase the contrasts in the size of the figures, which are scattered about so as to enhance the tension, just as the light and shadow is used to increase the drama. Vasari, when in Venice, praised this picture as Tintoretto's finest work; Vasari disapproved of Tintoretto entirely and considered he had no knowledge of drawing to the point that he could find no better excuse than to say that he treated art as a joke. This uneasiness, and the incomprehension that Vasari was not the only critic to feel, seems to derive from Tintoretto's use of colour, for he used his colour, not as Titian and Veronese did – to amplify the splendour of their forms – but to create a mood, and one moreover of

83 TINTORETTO *Last Supper*, S. Trovaso, *c.* 15

tension and emotion. Emotion in Veronese appears but rarely – perhaps in such a work as the *Baptist preaching*, and then it is artistic emotion dependent on the play of strange and beautiful colour in an unusual composition; in Titian emotion does not begin to appear until he is getting old, and his zest is diminishing – for most of his life he was too assured and too sanguine in temperament for emotion. But with Tintoretto the emotion is always near the surface to be expressed through movement, taut composition, and cool, disturbing colour.

If one compares, for instance, the *Last Suppers* he painted at varying stages through his career, the way his thought changes becomes much clearer to understand. The one in S. Marcuola in Venice, painted in 1547, is a traditional rendering of the scene, with a centrally planned composition with groups of apostles exactly balanced on either side of Christ, and the outside of the scene closed by two allegorical figures personifying Faith and Charity. The *Last Supper* in S. Trovaso in Venice, painted about 1560 also has a central plan, in that Christ is in the middle, but the alignment has been exploded into a lozenge-shaped grouping, seen from above as if from a balcony, with the bursting out of the composition stressed by the overturned chair, and by the way some figures fling themselves away from the table, not for dramatic reasons inherent in the incidents of the Last Supper, but for contrived and trivial reasons such as reaching for more wine or another dish. In the background,

the brilliant daylight in the arcades shines behind Christ, and upon the bright columns against which Judas is darkly silhouetted; and a mysterious staircase rises from a gloomy corner into shadowy recesses above (*Pl. 83*).

Like Titian, Tintoretto kept a huge shop; no one could have got through all he painted without one. The system on which he worked was quite different from that in Titian's or Veronese's shop, in that he never kept his assistants to making copies or close versions of finished works, or even merely to the preparatory stages of his huge commissions, but used them to make enlargements of his sketches, and on extensively altered variants of his pictures. There was, therefore, more freedom and much less repetition, which is reflected in the immense variety of his *œuvre*. He sacked the works of others, too; the *Last Judgement* in S. Maria del'Orto contains whole figures lifted out of the Sistine Chapel *Last Judgement*, and also echoes it in the confused, fragmented arrangement. A work of this kind, like the enormous *Paradise* painted in 1584-87 for the largest hall in the Doge's Palace, or the huge *Battle of Zara* also painted for the palace in the same years, shows him striving for effects he could achieve easily, yet with them winning victories

84 TINTORETTO
*Discovery of the body
of St Mark*, 1562

TINTORETTO *Morosini*

which have added little to his fame. The works done for the State after the great fires of 1574 and 1577 in the palace account for the importance of his shop, and for his frank re-use of old compositions, reversed and slightly varied for new purposes.

In 1562 he was commissioned to paint three pictures from the Legend of St Mark for the Scuola Grande di S. Marco: *St Mark rescuing the Saracen*, the *Discovery of the body of St Mark* (*Pl. 84*), and the *Removal of St Mark's body*. All three display that constant quality of the subject being caught at the most sudden and fleeting moment; the saint jerking the sailor from among his companions in the rowing boat; the saint appearing to identify his body from among the many housed in the row of wall tombs suspended like balconies along the vaulted hall, with the extraordinary light appearing under the door rising like a shutter at the end of the hall to reveal grotesque little figures peering underneath; the violent thunderstorm miraculously provided to conceal the theft of the holy body from the storm-racked piazza where the ghostly little church rises like the folly in an eighteenth-century park to close the long vista plunging into space. He began working for the Scuola di S. Rocco soon after – in 1564. The confraternity held a competition to select an artist, but Tintoretto won by the unfair trick of painting the actual ceiling decoration and fixing it in place – a trick which made him many enemies, but secured him the commission for the whole of the decoration of the Scuola's vast halls, upstairs and down, and he worked for them for the rest of his life, painting his last work for them in 1588. During this time he was also constantly working for the State, for other confraternities, and for churches and monasteries. He also painted many portraits, though these exhibit much less inventiveness than Titian's, and are closer to Bassano's simple effigies. Yet none excelled him in the portrayal of old age (*Pl. 85*).

The Scuola di S. Rocco is on two floors, and has three rooms. On the walls of the small room – the Albergo, or council room— he painted the *Crucifixion* (*Pl. 86*), *Christ before Pilate*, and the *Road to Calvary* (*Pl. 87*), in an indescribable panorama filled with men and horses, soldiers, executioners, and crowds of curious onlookers, with a poignant group of the fainting Virgin collapsed in the exhaustion of grief and horror at the foot of the Cross. Between 1576 and 1581 he decorated the Upper Hall with the Life of Christ in

86 TINTORETTO *Crucifixion*, Scuola di S. Rocco, 1565, detail

huge canvases seventeen feet high, and from 1583 to 1587 he painted the Lower Hall with scenes from the Life of the Virgin, in canvases over twelve feet high. Unfortunately, later restoration has made these pictures dark and gloomy, where their original technique was filled with light and colour, but the extraordinary visionary effect

87 TINTORETTO *Road to Calvary*, Scuola di S. Rocco, 1566

88 TINTORETTO *Flight into Egypt*, Scuola di S. Rocco, detail

89 TINTORETTO *Flight into Egypt*, Scuola di S. Rocco, 1583-7

can be gauged from the moonlit landscape in the *Flight into Egypt*, where the fronds of the trees seem to be flung on to the canvas with strokes as broad and free as if housepainters' brushes had been used (*Pls. 88, 89*).

Occasionally he painted mythologies, though basically he was a religious painter. The *Venus, Mars, and Vulcan* (Munich) pokes fun at the classical story of adultery, and Mars, caught in his mistress's bedroom, hides under the bed; the *Muses* (Hampton Court) are an excuse for displaying his ability in painting the nude in the elegant *contrapposto* of central Italian Mannerism; the Doge's Palace decorations forced him to such mythologies as should glorify Venice, as well as enable him to compete with Veronese. At the end of his life he clearly, triumphantly, returned to the form of composition he had started with: the vast frieze composed in

110

90 TINTORETTO *Last Supper*, S. Giorgio Maggiore, 1592

zigzags, or with plunging perspectives, for of this kind are the canvases in S. Giorgio Maggiore, of the *Gathering of the Manna* and the *Last Supper* (*Pl. 90*), painted from 1592 until the year of his death in 1594. They are treated as mystic meals, type and antitype from Old and New Testament, the *Manna* filled with groups in rhythmic movements leading the eye backwards into the crowded distance beyond the trees, the *Last Supper* with the great table splitting the room diagonally, and dividing the apostles from the group of busy servants. The scene is irradiated by flickering light with a crowd of moving, turning figures, yet never loses, amid the complexity and restlessness, that dramatic and religious feeling, which is enhanced rather by the contrasts of the corporeality of the human beings and the ghostly angelic figures filling the upper air as if they emanated from the flaring lamp or from the unearthly radiance surrounding Christ. The apostles argue among themselves about the meaning of Christ's action in the institution of the Eucharist, and this treatment of the drama in the Upper Chamber as a vast religious ceremonial seen as a contemporary event illustrates not only the difference between Leonardo and Tintoretto, but is the measure of the changes in the religious and intellectual climate during the hundred years that separate the two representations of the *Last Supper*.

91 TINTORETTO *Entombment*, 1594

The last word is with the *Entombment* of 1594 (*Pl. 91*). In this
last work Tintoretto sums up the ideas that had first moved him,
and ends with a grandeur and a pathos that achieves his ambition
to combine Titian with Michelangelo, by equalling both and yet
transcending neither.

CHAPTER FOUR

The Renaissance in the North

FLANDERS

No one could pretend that the art of the Netherlands after the death of Hugo van der Goes in 1482 – with one or two exceptions – was of the interest and quality of the preceding half-century. The great generation of the van Eycks, Roger van der Weyden, Bouts and Hugo was succeeded by men who exploited much the same field, and whose works are full of charm, but, principally, they provide a lesson in the spread of ideas, in the indigestibility of many of those ideas, and in the mutations they underwent in the process of their adaptation. Neither Matsys nor Mabuse provide the sonorous majesty of Jan van Eyck, nor the deep pathos of Roger, nor the wilder, more heartrending emotion of Hugo. They are competent, lively, versatile, curious, with a keen eye ever open for what may be useful among the new ideas floating about in their world. Van Orley brings his immense competence to the building up of a successful business as an art-merchant; no order too small, prompt execution, high charges, only the best materials and workmen used. Lucas van Leyden comes near to greatness and genius, and almost as a bonus offers the nineteenth-century qualities of temperament and bohemianism. Gerard David, who lived on until 1521, was so imbued with the style and feeling of the fifteenth-century that although he knew the Italianate style of the new century – he could hardly have escaped doing so, since he lived in its home, Antwerp, from 1515 to 1521 – he remained almost totally unaffected by it. The one great genius is Bruegel.

Quentin Matsys looks forward where David looks back, so that the sixteenth-century style of the Antwerp Mannerists starts with him as its first major exponent. One of the reasons for the shift in style was economic. By the end of the fifteenth century Bruges and Ghent were declining towns, still rich and prosperous, though not what they had been in the heyday of the Burgundian empire. Antwerp, which in those days had been a mudflat fishing harbour, rose steadily in importance as a port because the canals upon which both Bruges and Ghent depended were not only silting up, but also because one of the consequences of the Portuguese maritime discoveries during the fifteenth century was a steady increase in the burthen of ships, for which they needed deeper anchorage. Antwerp, a deep-river port, was also a more useful Western seaboard terminal than the inland harbours of Ghent and Bruges, and, like London and Lisbon, it flourished on the slow but steady rise in trade from waters outside the Mediterranean. A further reason for its rise was the steady removal of foreign warehouses formerly centred on Ghent and Bruges, because of the more liberal trading policy of the Antwerp guilds, which were less monopolistic and less riven by bitter faction.

Quentin Matsys was born in Louvain in 1464/65, and died in Antwerp in 1530. Although he is known to have been established in Antwerp by 1491, the earliest certain date for a work is 1507, when the *St Anne* triptych was commissioned, and he signed and dated it in 1509 (*Pls. 92, 93*). The *St Anne* altar is very large – the centre panel is about 7 × 8 feet – and in subject it is essentially northern, for the Holy Kinship, based on a vision of a St Colette Boilet, a local saint who died in Ghent in 1447, became very popular in the second half of the fifteenth century in Flanders and Germany. In form it sticks to the traditional *sacra conversazione* type, and many details, such as the heavy draperies and the use of a landscape background, are reminiscent of the fifteenth century. But the colour is very different: pale, blond, light blue, clear, and very impressive in the use of these pallid tonalities, while the detail of, for instance, the little domed tabernacle with porphyry columns, the use of caricature types, suggests experiences outside the earlier Flemish repertory. The landscape itself is quite different. Gone are the quiet pastoral scenes of Bouts or Hugo; now the landscape is eventful, and full of lively details of craggy mountains, castles, horsemen, torrents and peaks. The new trend in landscape painting was dominant in the north for almost the whole of the century – until, in fact, the rise of the Dutch landscape painters in the seventeenth century, with their interest in the local scene. This change almost

92 MATSYS *St Anne* triptych, 1509

certainly reflects influences from abroad, for Patinier, who was a
strict contemporary of Matsys, displays an even more fantastic
form of it, derived partly from Italy – from Leonardo, Mantegna
and the Milanese – and partly from Germany – from Dürer, Altdorfer, Cranach and the Danube School. Dürer is the most likely
source, since he was readily available in engravings, but the currents
in these ideas are very involved indeed, since Florentines in the
mid-sixteenth century were also using the engravings of Dürer
and Lucas van Leyden, so that the influences work in a kind of
circle. But even in 1509, in the *St Anne* altar, or in Matsys's later
Lamentation triptych of 1511, there is still no attempt to treat the
central panel and the wings in a unified scheme, or even in one scale.
The figures chop and change position in the artist's created space
purely according to the needs of the story, and never because of
any inner logic. His concern is with surface enrichment, more elaborate detail, still-life interest, and contrasts in facial expressions and
gestures between the good and bad characters in his narratives.
There is no attempt to solve problems presented by crowds of
figures, for it is not unity or impact of an artistic kind that he is
striving for, but impact through the weight of narrative detail.

93 MATSYS Centre panel of *St Anne* triptych

In his portraits, Matsys is a far more organized artist. He uses
the forms and language of Roger or Memlinc, but gives more space
to his figures, more light and shadow to render the feeling of arrest-
ed movement, and wide, splendid landscapes in the background give
air and the sixteenth-century feeling for setting. Is this the repercussion of Italian example in the north, or is it derived once more

94 MATSYS *Money Changer and his Wife*, 1514

from Dürer, who, in any case, had twice been to Venice by this date? As well as the simple type of portrait represented by the *Canon*, Matsys created another kind: the genre type depicting a scholar in his study, of which the best examples are the *Egidius* at Longford Castle (*Pl. 96*), and the copy of a lost original of *Erasmus* in the Corsini Collection in Rome. This is an adaptation of the usual

iconography of a *St Jerome*, such as the one in Detroit, which is probably a late fifteenth-century copy of an original which may go back to Jan van Eyck, and for Erasmus would have the added point that he was the greatest of all Jerome's commentators. A letter from St Thomas More to Erasmus, dated 1517, mentions the portrait of Egidius, while Erasmus must have sat for his when on his way to Basle through Antwerp. Again, the influence of Dürer's engraving of *St Jerome in his Study* of 1514 is probably of more relevance to the development of this type in the north than, for instance, any remote knowledge of Antonello's *St Jerome*. The still-life clutter of shelves, books, and other paraphernalia as a setting for a portrait also has connections with Petrus Christus's *St Eligius as a Goldsmith*, which in turn links up with Matsys's *Money Changer and his Wife* (*Pls. 94, 95*), dated 1514, particularly in the little mirror on the table – a distant echo of Jan van Eyck's *Arnolfini* marriage portrait. The Banker or Money Changer picture in turn seems to have given rise to an interest in an extraordinary subject – that of Tax Gatherers. The most exaggerated versions of this are by Marinus van Reymerswaele, who was active between about 1509 and about 1567. No one has yet explained why these caricature types, commemorating one of life's less pleasant concerns, should have occurred at all, much less have become so popular that about thirty versions of it are known, but the taste for caricature and 'moral contrast' subjects also include examples like Matsys's *Ill-matched Pair* – a low-life genre scene descended from the iconogra-

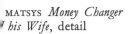

MATSYS *Money Changer*
his Wife, detail

96 MATSYS *Egidius*, 1517

97 MABUSE
Hercules and Dejanira, 1516

phy of the Prodigal Son, to become in turn the ancestor of the Flemish tavern picture. It is therefore possible that all these odd subjects contain a symbolism of the contrast between good and evil, or a moral example, the point of which may have been clearer then than it is now. But the interest in caricature and a rather equivocal moral lesson is important for the future.

If Matsys went to Italy, then it ought to have been before 1519, when he bought himself a house in Antwerp, frescoed the façade and put up a polychromed statue that made it one of the sights of the town. When Dürer came to Antwerp in 1520 he visited the house, but Matsys was away. Evidence that by this date copies of Leonardo were in circulation in the north is provided by the *Grotesque Woman* in the National Gallery, which was fairly certainly made from a Leonardo drawing now in Windsor, and stronger evidence is to be found in the *Madonna and Child* at Poznan (*Pl. 98*).

The omission here of the St Anne does not disguise its derivation from Leonardo's *St Anne* cartoon in the Louvre, but this divorce between the main figures, and the substitution of a typical Flemish landscape, suggests that the copy was only a fragmentary one. Though the basic idea is recognizably Italian, the language is a borrowed one, and stems neither from his previous work nor from what one can assess as his own mental processes. It is a Fleming speaking Italian with a strong native accent, not the outcome of the thought, tradition and training which formed the artist.

Jan Gossaert is called Mabuse because he came from Maubeuge; he was in the Antwerp guild by 1503, but a work such as the large *Adoration* (*Pl. 100*) in the National Gallery, London is so old-fashioned in its fifteenth-century outlook – high viewpoint, mystery play narrative, indecisions of scale in the angels, and a *horror vacui* accumulation of fantastic detail – that it is probably his master work and dates from about 1503-6. In 1508 he went to Rome, which means that he was there immediately before the revolution effected by the major works of Michelangelo and Raphael. At first, he continues much as before, for the *Madonna and Child* in Palermo has all the flamboyance of German woodcarver's Gothic, mixed with *putti*

98 MATSYS
Madonna and Child, c. 1527

derived from Ferrarese paintings of the 1480s. Then he realized
that the things he had seen were unknown in the north, and quite
suddenly he changed completely. He began to produce pictures
which mix in the strangest manner the kind of draperies and attitudes of traditional northern painting, with Italianate architectural
features at first incorporating late Gothic details, as in the *St Luke
painting the Virgin* (*Pl. 99*), of about 1514 in Prague, and then by

100 MABUSE *Adoration of the Magi*, 1503-6

123

MABUSE *St Luke painting the Virgin, c.* 1514

about 1518, in another version of the subject in Vienna, becoming as Italianate as possible, with details inspired by an uneasy mixture of Botticelli, Mantegna, Fra Bartolommeo and Filippino Lippi, with architectural fantasies of a Milanese character. The result is a florid, mannered, rather nightmarish style, in which nothing essential is assimilated and only the externals imitated. He also introduced a different kind of secular subject: classical mythologies. The *Hercules and Amphitrite* in Berlin, signed and dated 1516, is heavily dependent for the figures upon Dürer's *Adam and Eve* print of 1504 and there are other instances such as a *Hercules and Dejanira* (*Pl. 97*), and a *Danäe*, as well as drawings of the Spinario and an hermaphrodite statue. It would not be worth instancing examples of such Italianisms if the particular could not be made to furnish a generalization: it is that when northern artists suffered the impact of Italian art, it was necessary for them to be very great geniuses – like Dürer or Bruegel – if their independence was to survive, and in 1516 or '17, a major work by Raphael arrived in Brussels, for the Sistine Chapel tapestries were woven there and the cartoons remained in Flanders afterwards.

In his own day, Bernard van Orley was called the Raphael of the North, which speaks rather more for Raphael's fame than it does for northern judgement. He was born in Brussels about 1488, and

101 VAN ORLEY *Georg van Zelle*, 1519

102 VAN ORLEY *Trials of Job*. Centre panel, 1532

103 VAN ORLEY *Dives and Lazarus*. From wings of *Job* altarpiece

104 RAIMONDI *Massacre of the Innocents*. Engraving after Raphael

died there in 1541. His principal patrons were successive Regents of the Netherlands, Margaret of Austria and Mary of Hungary, the first an aunt, and the second a sister of the Emperor Charles V, so that the familiarity of the patron with Italian work of the finest kind is also to be reckoned with as a factor in the spread of Italianism

105 LUCAS VAN LEYDEN *Magdalen returning to the World*. Woodcut, 1519

in the north. Van Orley is at his best in portraits – such as the splendid 'scholar in his study' one of *Georg van Zelle* (*Pl. 101*) dated 1519 – and in his tapestries, which both reflect his experience of Raphael, and disseminate Italianism. In his major altarpiece, the *Trials of Job* (*Pl. 102*), dated 1532, in Brussels, the central panel of the destruction of Job's children, and all except one small part of the wings, which contain the story of Dives and Lazarus (*Pl. 103*), have only the sort of references to Italian art that would be got from hearsay – Job's stricken children remind one of, but are not copied from, Signorelli's *Fall of Antichrist* in Orvieto, and the architecture in all the scenes has the type of dumpy marble column and Milanese panels and friezes of grotesques that Mabuse also used. The narrative is very vehement: Dives at his feast, the beggar expiring at his gate, the death of Dives, and his plea in

106 SCOREL *Magdalen*

Hell for a drop of water to ease his thirst. But who is this unhappy sinner? Is he not Heliodorus, lying beneath the hoofs of the avenging angel's horse? And how does he come to be Heliodorus, rather than Ananias from the Cartoons?

The other great factor, besides the firsthand exposure through travel to Italy, and contact with imported works, was by means of engravings. The frontispieces of books, so frequently incorporating architectural motives, illustrated Books of Hours with decorative borders, illustrated editions of Herodotus, Petrarch, Lives of the Saints, that came in increasing volume from Italian, particularly Venetian, presses, were one of the means of diffusion, and artist's prints – those of Mantegna in particular, and of other Mantuan, Venetian, Ferrarese, and Florentine engravers and the celebrated plate by Bramante – were probably even more important because they would have had more authority. But most important of all were the engravings of Marcantonio Raimondi, who was born about 1480, worked in Venice as a forger of Dürer's prints, and then moved to Rome about 1510 where he became the principal diffuser of ideas and works emanating from Raphael and his circle (*Pl. 104*). After the Sack he returned to Bologna, and there disappears from view. He was extremely prolific: over three-hundred engravings are known, and these spread all over Europe not only the works of Raphael and his school, but antique sculptures, fantastic allegories, portraits, mythologies, genre scenes by many hands. To these must be added the works of Dürer, Cranach, Urs Graf, and Lucas van Leyden.

Lucas was reported to have been extremely precocious – a competent painter at fifteen – that is, by about 1510. He spent most of his time in Leyden, and married a rich woman there in 1515, which may account for some of his later vagaries. Dürer visited him in 1520, and he went on a short journey with Mabuse in 1527, when he entertained local artists lavishly, perhaps in imitation of Dürer during his Netherlandish journey in 1520-21. He died fairly young – about 1533 – and believed himself to have been poisoned by his rivals, whom he avoided by working in bed. There are few paintings, but his output of woodcuts (*Pl. 105*) was large enough to suggest that he was a busy, though not prolific artist, although this accords ill with the dilettante picture of the travelling, the lying in bed, the wining and dining in yellow silk clothes. His paintings have the most beautiful fluid brushwork, the soft, loaded brush squiggling with a liquid calligraphic line, and wonderful colour; not surprising as Matsys's *St Anne* is, by its all-over pallor and blueness, but surprising in detail. Green shadows, mauve shadows, little flushed patches of pink or pale greeny-blue, so that flesh has an almost impressionist quality of colour, and then into the melting variety of tint he drops a firm incisive line, a hard edge flicked in and out with consummate mastery (*Pl. 107*). His woodcuts can be dated from 1510 on, which, if he was truly born in 1494, makes his youthful performance very impressive indeed. Many of his subjects are close to Dürer's, and sometimes also to Schongauer, with great play made with the draperies in rather archaic systems of folds. Sometimes they are additions to the inventive iconography of the north; sometimes he brings to his woodcuts the virtuoso qualities of line of his best paintings, or grades the thickness of his line according to the depth in space – a hallmark of the very best Dürer technique.

The temper of the mid-century is shown by an artist like Jan Scorel, who travelled all over Germany, and into Italy, went to

107 LUCAS VAN LEYDEN
Sermon in a Church

108 BRUEGEL *Parable of the Blind*, 1568

Jerusalem on a pilgrimage, arrived back in Venice in 1521, made his fortune by being in Rome at the right moment to be practically the only artist patronized by the Dutch pope Hadrian VI, came back to Utrecht full of the influences of Giorgione, Palma Vecchio, Raphael and Michelangelo, and later went to France. At his worst, he is a self-conscious imitator; at his best, he has a striking gift for vivid characterization in rich and evocative colour (*Pl. 106*). The drawings of his pupil, Maerten van Heemskerck, made in Rome in 1532-35, are among the most vivid and important records of the state of St Peter's and of Roman antiquities in those years, and the style he brought back with him combines Italian fluency and spaciousness with northern realism – particularly in his fine portraits – and also with deliberate Italianisms designed to impress his patrons.

The south became such a magnet that Bruegel, immediately after he became a member of the Antwerp Guild in 1551, set off on a journey that took him across France and down through Italy as far as Sicily. He was in Rome in 1553, and returned across the Alps about 1554 (*Pl. 110*). This long and arduous journey had a considerable influence on his development of new forms in landscape, while the art of Italy seems to have had almost no impact at all. After his return, he began working for engravers on popular prints, and the kind of terror-fantasies that Bosch had specialized in. He then evolved an entirely new subject matter in his pictures based on proverbs; he adapted the ideas of the inner meanings of the still-life, gestures, and setting in religious pictures to a new iconography of moral significance based on the illustration of everyday life and manners. Sometimes entirely fantastic, like the *Dulle Griet* (*Pl. 112*) or the *Triumph of Death*, but more often either entirely realistic, like the *Wedding Feast*, or hovering on the borderline between reality and a dreamworld, like the *Land of Cockaigne*, or the *Parable of the Blind*

109 BRUEGEL *Magpie and the Gallows*, 1568

110 BRUEGEL *Alpine Scenery*. Drawing, *c.* 1552/4

111 BRUEGEL *Stormy Day*, 1565

(*Pl. 108*), these pictures are sermons on the vices and follies of mankind, and were recognized and prized as such in the painter's lifetime. In his last ten years (he died in 1569) he produced vast landscapes based ultimately on the experiences of his Alpine journey (*Pl. 111*), often with this moral content, like the *Magpie and the Gallows* (*Pl. 109*), but also, in the great series of the *Months*, all but one of which is dated 1565, with the profounder thesis of the unity of mankind and nature. Far from being the simple, earthy character suggested by the nickname 'Peasant', Pieter Bruegel was a man of erudition, the friend of humanists, and greatly appreciated by an enlightened patron, Cardinal Granvelle, Philip II's minister in the Netherlands.

His contemporaries meanwhile bogged down in the imitation of Italian forms in all too literal a sense. Painters like Aertsen and Bueckelaer converted their vast still-lifes of market and kitchen scenes into religious pictures by disguising the background figures

112 BRUEGEL *Dulle Griet*, 1564

113 BUECKELAER *Christ in the House of Martha and Mary*, 1565

114 FLORIS *Last Judgement*, 1565

as Christ in the house of Martha and Mary (*Pl. 113*), or the Prodigal Son. More usually, the realism is confined to sober and often sensitive portraits, like those of the Pourbus family, while the subject pictures – such as those by Martin de Vos, Floris (*Pl. 114*), and the members of the Pourbus family in their grand manner moments – become the battlefield of Raphael-inspired idealism and Michelangelo-inspired nudes, with a consequent incoherence of style. They adopt Italian ideas and forms, but are necessarily lacking in the classical tradition which made the development of those ideas natural in the south, so that they are merely a matter of fashion, of using the up-to-date language. Ideas from Leonardo, such as the Leda twisted pose, and the smoky *sfumato* modelling; ideas from Raphael, derived from the Cartoons, through Marcantonio, from school works imported into the north; fragments of Michelangelo's *terribilità*. In architecture, they were so conditioned by the florid quality of late Gothic that the simplicity and severity of the best Renaissance work was ignored in favour of the confused and fantasticated Certosa at Pavia, or the elaboration of the courtyard of the Doge's Palace in Venice. The term Flemish, or Antwerp, Mannerism is a useful, but also a confusing one, convenient as a label to distinguish the art of this epoch from earlier Flemish painting; yet there is really nothing Mannerist about it at all. Mannerism, properly, can only refer to Italian art, in the sense that it is a result of, and a sequel to, High Renaissance forms and ideas. The north merely adopts the vocabulary, as the outward sign of an admired and coveted standard of education and culture, but the inner meaning of the language is a closed book. Only a few men, like Dürer, Bruegel and Holbein understood the gulf.

FRANCE

The importance of the sudden emergence of the School of Fontainebleau is because its repercussions reached far beyond the place from which it takes its name. It became a main centre for the diffusion of Italian Renaissance ideas in northern Europe, because instead of a slow permeation of northern art by ideas from Italy, the new style sprang from the direct patronage of Francis I with the completeness of Minerva springing fully armed from Jupiter's head. Though there had been hints during the mid-fifteenth century of Italian ideas in the miniaturists and tombmakers, by the turn of the century the invasion of France by Italian forms was as overwhelming as the military invasions of Italy by the French, of which they were the direct result. The French invasions of 1494 and 1499, which opened northern eyes to the splendour of Italian life and art, resulted particularly in the importation of Milanese forms, since Milan was the city they controlled for the longest time. The cluttered, confused, over-decorated Certosa of Pavia accorded well with the elaborate forms of Late Gothic current in the north, but under Francis I quite another attitude prevailed. His view of kingship, and the role for which he cast himself in European politics, was that of a dominant central power, and he required a courtly magnificence as a suitable setting for his position. Italian luxury, splendour and art were not just attractive in themselves; they were things which would put him on a par with other monarchs – if not actually enable him to excel them. To this end, he imported such major artists as he could; Michelangelo he failed to obtain, but he did get the ageing Leonardo. Rosso he imported in 1520, Primaticcio in 1532; Niccolò dell'Abbate, Vignola, Serlio, Andrea del Sarto, Cellini, all came; some stayed, some went back; but the work they left behind was decisive in that from this 'infection' from Italian sources Gothic died, to be replaced at first with hybrid and garbled forms of Italianism.

Only prestige came of Francis's capture of Leonardo; but in Rosso the king acquired an artist of ability, whose acute sufferings at the time of the Sack of Rome had exacerbated an already highly strung temperament. Primaticcio was at first overshadowed by his compatriot, but after Rosso's mysterious death in 1540, he came into his own and reigned supreme for the rest of his long life. Sarto's brief unhappy stay had little more effect than Cellini's stormy one; Vignola, who was in France for about eighteen months in the early 1540s at the very beginning of his career, never had the influence of the far less intelligent, but more accommodating Serlio. Between them, however, they prepared the ground for an impetus which was to be naturalized by the end of the century, and which would provide the forcing ground for the greatness of French seventeenth-century art. Rosso from a background of the Volterra *Deposition*, Primaticcio from the Palazzo del Tè, brought

115 PRIMATICCIO
Stucco decoration at
Fontainebleau, *c.* 1541-5

with them, not the serene art of Raphael or of Michelangelo's
Sistine Ceiling, but the conflict and obscurity, the contortion, tension and complexity of the years which saw the Sack.

Francis concentrated his patronage on the decoration of the
Château of Fontainebleau, and this decoration is the keynote of the
new style. Painted allegories, mythologies, histories, all extolling the
glory of the King, were framed by figures, trophies, garlands, cut
leather panels, *putti*, executed in stucco in a relief so high as to be
almost free standing (*Pl. 115*). The figures are tall, slender, elegant;
the garlands and strapwork intertwine so that the frame is more
vivid and splendid than the picture enclosed in it. Tapestries of
similar type, easel pictures concentrating on the all-important female
nude, portraits emulating the elegance of Bronzino's Medici court
portraits, imaginary landscapes with enormous panoramas of mountain ranges and shadowy cities peopled by the characters of mythol-
ogy like tiny puppets against a fantastic backcloth, religious pictures with involved imagery and tortured *contrapposto*, even the
minor arts of miniatures, jewellery, textiles, all show the impact of
Fontainebleau, and that search for luxuriance and sophistication
which is the hallmark of Francis's court.

116 COUSIN *Eva Prima Pandora*, c. 1538

117 NICCOLÒ DELL'ABBATE *Orpheus and Eurydice*

8 CLOUET *Pierre Quthe*, 1562

119 CLOUET *Lady in her Bath,*
c. 1550

The Fontainebleau decorations included a Long Gallery, a Ballroom, and rooms for the king, the queen, and the king's mistress, the Duchesse d'Étampes. Only a fraction survives, since much was destroyed in later rebuildings, and most of the paintings were drastically restored in the nineteenth century. The wonderful stucco figures framing the mutilated pictures have a curious ancestry, for they are a three-dimensional form of the painted friezes of fictive sculpture in, for instance, Giulio Romano's Sala di Costantino decorations, or the dado of caryatid figures painted by Perino del Vaga under the frescoes in the Stanze to replace the inlaid woodwork destroyed during the Sack. After Rosso's death, Primaticcio continued without a major collaborator until the arrival about 1552 of Niccolò dell'Abbate (*Pl. 117*). His main contribution was his fantastic landscapes, which are a genre quite apart from either the poetic realism found in late fifteenth-century Italian pictures, or the homely kind in the background of the Raphael Cartoons. They have a dreamlike quality with extremes of light and colour, rainbows and flickering storms: odes with the impact of incantations. This feeling for mood in landscape is not entirely new, since it can be found in earlier works inspired from different

140

sources. The *Eva Prima Pandora* (*Pl. 116*), painted by Jean Cousin the Elder about 1538, shows the result of Rosso and Cellini in the nude figure, but the rocky landscape of the grotto and the open vista beyond betray more than a nodding acquaintance with Leonardo and the engravings of the Danube school of landscape painters. One of the difficulties besetting French painting at this moment is the diversity of influences to which it was open.

In portraits a whole gallery of new sources is obvious: the *Pierre Quthe* (*Pl. 118*) of 1562 by François Clouet is patently influenced by Bronzino's court portraits, and also by Holbein and the Pourbus family in Flanders. These same influences blend in the *Lady in her Bath* (*Pl. 119*), probably Marie Touchet, mistress of Charles IX who died in 1574 at the age of twenty-four. This is the classic portrayal of a Royal mistress in her official role, cool, beautiful, aloof, bejewelled even in her bath, accompanied by the trappings of her state – fine rooms, a noble child in the arms of its leering, accomplice-nurse, the sly Love-child stealing the fruits, the flower of passion in her hand. Yet the influence of the *Mona Lisa* is there

120 Master of Flora *Birth of Cupid, c.* 1540/60

too, for this picture seems to have accompanied Leonardo to France, and many versions – some close to the original, some virtually parodies – exist, with nude versions rather more popular than the reticent original. There was also a market for evocations of the Raphael 'Mistress' portrait – the nude, bejewelled *Fornarina* which it is so hard to credit to Raphael himself, despite, and perhaps because of, the blatant signature – tricked out in classical trappings so as to combine provocativeness with the respectability of a learned language. The Bronzino *Venus, Cupid, Time and Folly* (*Pl. 33*), sent to Francis I by Cosimo I, was undoubtedly one of the main vehicles for the introduction into France of the erotic nude, with steely draughtsmanship, and hauntingly frigid colour. And the Bronzino version of Michelangelo's cartoon of Leda, itself descended from the *Night* of the Medici tombs, crossed with influences from Correggio's and Titian's *Danäe* subjects, crossed in turn with Primaticcio's stucco figures brings the wheel full circle in a work such as the Master of Flora's *Birth of Cupid* (*Pl. 120*). Primaticcio's art, in fact, remained the most potent, since it was the longest, and the readiest available, translation of Italian art into French.

But to introduce new ideas at a central point of diffusion, and to engender by their means a new indigenous school are quite different things. The second generation of native French artists at Fontainebleau produced no men of the quality of Rosso and Primaticcio. Too often they were attracted by the showy and fantastic elements in their Italian models, such as extremes of perspective and *outré* colour, and too many works founder in confused form and in an overt eroticism which implies only a superficial understanding of the true nature of Renaissance art. The Wars of Religion put an end to nearly all patronage in the later years of the century, and when the arts began to revive under Henry IV the original Fontainebleau sources were still drawn on, plus the Flemish Italianizers who imported still further distortions into what they took from Italy. People like Ambroise Dubois, a Fleming who settled in France, where he died in 1614, or Toussaint Dubreuil, who died in 1602, continue the fantastic distortions, the erotic nude; but the spark is dead, and the weak drawing, and the confusions of space and scale, mask the poverty of imagination and style. Only Antoine Caron, who died in 1600, still impresses as an extreme of sophisticated court art;

121 CARON *The Massacres of the Triumvirate*, 1566

his pictures look like gigantic ballets, and were probably inspired by them, for ballet was one of the great amusements of the court of Catherine de' Medici, the queen-mother, and his chief patron (*Pl.121*).

Francis I's third important acquisition was Sebastiano Serlio. He was a Bolognese, born in 1475 – which makes him considerably older than Rosso or Primaticcio – who had been in Rome as an assistant to Peruzzi, who was himself one of Bramante's men. After the Sack, he went to Venice and there began to work on an illustrated treatise for the use of architects and their patrons. He dedicated one of the volumes to Francis I in 1540, and was then invited to France and given the control of the building works at Fontaine-bleau. His treatise eventually became a major work with an impact enhanced by the fact that he sprang, so to speak, from the fountain-head. That he had been unable to compete in Venice with Sansovino should have suggested something; but in the new climate of France, passionate interest in Italian art was coupled with naïve ignorance and inexperienced taste. Serlio's tactful suggestions for the conversion of old-fashioned Gothic houses into modern Ital-

143

122 SERLIO Frontispiece to Book V (first published 1547) of 'Dieci Libri'

ianate palaces, and his showy designs for gateways, staircases, chimney pieces, which – however far they departed from what an educated Italian would have built – were believed to be examples of the pure, new fashion derived from antiquity, were received with welcoming approbation. His books were best-sellers; Dutch, German, English editions (books One to Five, 'by Sebastian Serly', London 1611, were from the Dutch edition) spread Serlio's version of Italian Renaissance architecture all over Europe (*Pl. 122*). His buildings in France were very few and his influence was utterly disproportionate to his attainments. The curious thing is that he found a market at all, since he had to compete with Lescot and Philibert de l'Orme, both of whom had a far better understanding of the Italian style than he had, and, in the case of Philibert, was an architect of genius who worked for three years in Italy.

Very little survives of Primaticcio's buildings; the grotto at Fontainebleau of about 1543 is typical of the fantasy architecture inherited from Giulio Romano – massive piers with figures of imprisoned giants incorporated into the rustication, derived from the Michelangelo *Slaves* of which the pair now in the Louvre were owned by the Connétable de Montmorency at Écouen by 1546. By

123 LESCOT Cour Carrée, Louvre, begun 15

1568, the date of the wing known as the 'Aile de la Belle Cheminée', Primaticcio is far closer to Vignola who was by that time the most important representative of the new Academic movement, a combination of the 'back-to-Bramante' trend with the reaction against Giulio Romano's waywardness, which he would have known about from his visit to Italy in 1563.

Pierre Lescot, who was born about the turn of the century and died in 1578, was not – as was usually the case – trained as a mason, but received a learned education and may even have been to Rome in his youth, though his only certain visit was in 1556, too late to affect his architecture. His great surviving work is at the Louvre, where the keep was demolished to make space for a square court which he began in 1546. Later the project was doubled in size to form the present Cour Carrée, though this larger scheme was not carried out until well into the seventeenth century. His buildings, at the south-east corner of the courtyard, are very classical, with pure

proportions and excellent detail, ornamental but with real under-standing of the orders (*Pl. 123*). He retains the common form of the 'frontispiece' – that is, the surviving idea of the towered gateway – treated as an important feature on the central axis of the building, but this traditional shape is rationalized into new combinations. The detailing is superb, with very high quality sculpture, probably by Jean Goujon, who also created, with Lescot, the large Salle des Caryatides, where the gallery is borne on female figures, according to a form described by Vitruvius. The other great sculptor of the period was Germain Pilon. Basically, his inspiration derives from the Fontainebleau stuccoes, but he develops a wonderfully flowing movement, which is deeply expressive (*Pl. 127*).

In Philibert de l'Orme, France produced the first northern archi-tect fit to stand among the great Italians. He was born in Lyons about 1505/10, the son of a mason, and came to Paris about 1540 – that is, about the time that Serlio arrived. His first work after this was the country house of S. Maur-lès-Fossés, near Paris, now de-stroyed. This was not unlike the Palazzo del Te in design, being four-square round a court but with a double storey articulated by a

124 PHILIBERT Interior of Chapel at Anet, 1549-52   125 Frontispiece, Anet, 1549-52

126 PHILIBERT Gateway at Anet, 1552

giant order for the main block – the first appearance of a properly designed Order, and certainly of a giant order, in the north. Philibert also designed Anet for Diane de Poitiers, the mistress of Henri II, though only the gateway and the chapel remain on the site, and the central frontispiece has survived by being built into the École des Beaux-Arts in Paris (*Pl. 125*). This is another example of the old medieval gate-tower lingering on to be rationalized into the new systems by a sequence of orders properly in proportion, one above the other. The gateway at Anet achieves its decorative effects by purely architectural means, using blocks of masonry and balustraded terraces to create masses of light and shadow, so that the fanciful devices of clockwork hounds and stag at bay on the top, and the Cellini *Nymph* that once filled the tympanum, fall into their proper places as adjuncts to an architectural system (*Pl. 126*). The chapel is centrally planned, with all walls, pediments, doorways, windows and interior barrel vaulting following the curves of the

147

127 PILON *Deposition.* Relief, *c.* 1580/5

outside walls, while inside it is articulated by a superbly proportioned Corinthian order, with a beautifully cut inscription as the only decoration in the frieze, and the spirally coffered dome is reflected in the inlaid pattern of the floor (*Pl. 124*). This is no longer – and the date is in the early 1550s – a mere imitation of the superficial effects of Italian forms, such as Serlio dealt in. Philibert's two treatises on architecture, written during the years after his royal patron's death in 1559 and continued until his own death in 1570, when he was suffering the disgrace which resulted largely from his own arrogance during his period of favour, are not only manuals of instruction for the professional, but are valuable for their insistence on theory, so that they offer to architect and patron alike a means of achieving Sir Henry Wootton's famous dictum on architecture: 'firmnesse, commoditie, and delight.'

Before the French invasions of Italy the main art of the north had been architecture. It still remained so, though there is a case for arguing that the death of Gothic was a major loss, not compensated for by the ill-conceived forms of Renaissance by which it was initially superseded, for these amounted to little more than the addition of new style ornament to Gothic forms, in the belief that Renaissance art was nothing but an alternative kind of decoration. With men like Lescot and Philibert de l'Orme, or Goujon and Germain Pilon (*Pl. 127*), this belief gave place rapidly to a grasp of the fact that Italian art is fundamentally a matter of form and proportion. Painting expanded from an art previously confined to manuscript illumination, altarpieces, small devotional works, little portraits, into a monumental art. Huge schemes of decoration, like that at Fontainebleau, were exceptional, but the introduction of new subject matter – that is, the secularizing of painting through the development of alternatives to religious pictures, the increased scope possible in landscape and portraiture – reflects the general widening of intellectual horizons which is the special achievement of the Renaissance. The Renaissance painter, like his contemporary in scholarship, enabled the man of his time to stand outside himself and look at himself, his achievements, and the world about him, in a spirit of enquiry and detachment; it enabled him to create an image of himself. It made him conscious of himself, enlarged his stature, gave him dignity and self-confidence. The impact of the Renaissance in Fontainebleau may seem, when one looks at the dwindling lamps that the bright Italian lights became, but a poor end for so much hope and effort, but the world of Philibert de l'Orme is really the true moment of the birth of the Renaissance in the north. It was in this new world that Poussin and Philippe de Champaigne were introduced to an art founded on the Italian classics. And within twenty-five years this seed would be like the mustard tree of the parable.

GERMANY

Dürer so overshadowed his contemporaries that it is sometimes difficult to realize that he was dead by 1528, and that for about a quarter of a century afterwards most German artists only reflect a small portion of his achievements, and rarely escape his influence. One of the facets of his art is sometimes developed a little further in invention and expression, as the so-called Danube School painters did in landscape. In fact, the term Danube School is a complete misnomer, in that it was never a 'school' in the sense of a group of artists working together with a common aim. The members of it were contemporary, but there was little or no contact between them, and only two of them were in any way connected with the Danube. Roughly, the painters usually grouped under this head

128 CRANACH *Rest on the Flight,* 1504

are Cranach the Elder, who worked mostly in Wittenberg for the Electors of Saxony, Altdorfer who worked in Regensburg, and Wolf Huber, and only the last two have anything to do with the Danube. What they all have in common is a feeling for landscape, not just a background, but as a subject in itself, and they share also a predilection for large, shaggy fir trees, which make an expressive – even romantic – effect.

Lucas Cranach, who was born in 1472, was in Vienna probably from 1500 onwards, and in 1505 went to Wittenberg to become court painter to the Elector Frederick the Wise, who was also one of Dürer's patrons. He had already developed his landscape interests by 1503, for a *Crucifixion* of that year combines landscape with a mixture of late Gothic emotion and the imagery of Dürer, and by 1504 his *Rest on the Flight* (*Pl. 128*) has developed a full scale Dürer quality in the figures with the marvellously evocative forest scene, including the curious tattered fir tree. As a portrait painter he had nothing to learn from Dürer – witness the grand *Cuspinian* portraits of 1504-5 (*Pls. 130, 131*) – and he always sets his sitter with the amplitude and feeling for personality – the anti-effigy quality – of the best northern artists, perhaps Matsys as well as Dürer.

150

129 CRANACH *Judgement of Paris, c. 15⅝*

130 CRANACH *Dr Johannes Cuspinian, 1504-5*   131 CRANACH *Anna Cuspinian, 1504-5*

The result of the large workshop his court patronage forced him to establish was to make him unadventurous, formally stylized, with overtones of a very odd sophistication. He made history in that full-length portraits, not connected with religious subjects as donors, seem to be his invention. *Duke Henry of Saxony*, and *Duchess Katherine* are dated 1514 (*Pls. 132, 133*), but both are highly formalized, almost heraldic effigies, with a lifeless, signboard quality, and nothing of the space and colour of the superb Cuspinian pair. In the portrait of Cardinal Albrecht of Brandenburg, painted in 1527, the sitter is portrayed in the now-fashionable 'scholar-in-his-study' setting, but has only a minimal return to the feeling and movement of his early style. After the beginning of the 1520s, Cranach became interested – and, more unfortunately, so did his patrons – in mythological subjects of a pseudo-humanist type, and from then on come the series of Venuses, some betraying more clearly than others their origins in Venetian art. The *Sleeping Venus* of 1518, the *Judgement of Paris* of about 1530 (*Pl. 129*), stress not only the narrow confines of the workshop but a curious blend of erotic curiosity and undercover sensuality. Cranach was a lifelong friend of Luther; the best portraits of Luther are by him, and he made propaganda prints for him. But one of the results of the Reformation was to alter the type of religious painting. Certain subjects remained: the Old Testament ones, part of the Passion such as the Crucifixion, and subjects which combined religious with moral lessons, such as the Woman taken in Adultery, or Christ among the Children; but the old range of the Life of the Virgin, or of the Saints, the *sacra conversazione*, the miracle subject, had gone, and the humanist-cum-classical matter had to fill the gap. Hence the spate of Venuses, some entirely nude, some merely made naked by the addition of necklaces, wisps of transparent veiling and huge cartwheel hats. They were immensely popular, and highly prized all over the north as *objects de vertu*, evidence of culture and learning. Cranach also made many engravings, and illustrated a Lutheran bible, but technically his engravings are not in Dürer's class. His etchings – a new development in graphic art that Dürer had only touched on in passing – combine

132 CRANACH
Duke Henry of Saxony,
1514

133 CRANACH
Duchess Katherine, 1514

134 ALTDORFER *St George*, 1510

the Danube School landscape with something of Dürer's tradition, and are probably the best part of his graphic work. Some of his late portraits approach the early *Cuspinian* pair, and are important in that by this time portraiture had also become one of the outlets for patronage in the north, to replace religious art. There is a good

35 ALTDORFER *Christ taking leave of His Mother, c.* 1517

deal of confusion between the works of the elder Cranach and those of his workshop, and his sons: Hans who predeceased him in 1537 (Cranach the Elder died in 1553), and Lucas II who lived until 1586, particularly in the 'court' subjects and the more hack portraits.

Altdorfer was a Bavarian born about 1480, who lived until 1538. He seems to have settled in Regensburg about 1505, and eventually became city architect and a town councillor. Regensburg is on the Danube, and in 1511 – and probably earlier as well – he travelled down the river and then south into the Alps, where the scenery moved him so deeply that he became the first landscape painter in the modern sense. His earliest pictures show poetic imagination and a strong sense of mood, and they also have something of the best of Dürer and early Cranach. In the tiny *St George* of 1510 the landscape has become all important, and the figure of the saint is lost amid the thick forest (*Pl. 134*). Altdorfer's figures are invariably the complement of his romantic landscapes; for them he borrows from Dürer's inventive iconography, but the panoramic setting is personal, and has nothing to do with the fantasy landscapes of the Netherlanders. His greatest work is the Florian altar of 1518, most of which is still in the monastery, near Linz, for which it was painted.

136 ALTDORFER *Recovery of the body of St Florian*. Florian altar, 1518

137 HUBER *The Danube Valley*, 1529

The main part consists of a central portion of four panels in two
tiers, and two wings of two panels one above the other, painted
on both sides. Inside is the Passion, and the wings have scenes from
the martyrdoms of St Sebastian and St Florian (*Pl. 136*). Some of
the panels have a curiously visionary narrative quality – all the details seem sharpened and the emotional aspect heightened by a tangle
of weeds hanging from a wall, by bare boughs against the sky, by a
flaring, lurid sunrise, or a sunset of scarlet and gold suffused with
dark purplish stormclouds above deep green cliffs and forests. He
uses distortion in his forms and exaggeration in gesture and expression to produce dramatic and powerful emotional effects, and the
colour serves the same end, so that in the *Battle of Alexander the
Great* of 1529 he involves all nature in the conflict in a vast panorama, pale citron to blood red, with gold and purple and dusky
shadows, and cold, gleaming lights on the water and the hills.

138 AMBERGER
Christoph Fugger, 1541

This is much closer to the northern type of fantasy landscape, while at the same time it recalls Leonardo's cosmic visions of alpine storms and cataclysms. It is a different kind of thing from the passionate observation of nature found in his smaller pictures, where the landscapes can only have been painted for the love of rendering the effect of light on stone and verdure, and the strange shapes of tattered trees. Occasionally, an Italian detail crops up – the architecture in some of his Florian panels is derived from Bramante's famous engraving, some show even more wild fantastication than the Certosa, and this again is probably derived from books, though here and there a figure is so like Mantegna as to suggest that his alpine views were a result of travelling into northern Italy, from whence he returned with ideas that furnished his imagination with vividly new forms.

Wolf Huber was probably his assistant at some time around 1510, sharing his feeling for poetic landscape, particularly in his drawings, which have no subject but the vast panoramas of mountains, forests and sky (*Pl. 137*). The other great centre of patronage was Augsburg, which was the seat of the Imperial court. Hans Burgkmair and Jörg Breu, the elder Holbein, Strigel, and a little later Amberger (*Pl. 138*), Georg Pencz and Seisenegger, principally portrait painters, are the core of the Augsburg painters, and men upon whom Dürer had less influence than the direct impact of Italy, particularly Venice after the Emperor Charles V began to buy pictures by Titian. Burgkmair, Breu and the elder Holbein painted mainly religious pictures, the other men settled mainly for portraits, now bulking almost as large as woodcuts in artists' output. Burgkmair visited Italy several times, and imports into Augsburg a strong north Italian flavour (*Pl. 139*), while Holbein the Elder sticks closely to late Gothic traditions, with a haphazard Italianism derived from Burgkmair working through his flaccid forms. It is not for his own works that he is interesting, but because his large shop was the forcing-ground for his extraordinary son.

Hans Holbein the Younger was born in Augsburg in 1497/98, and, with his brother Ambrosius, who died in 1519, was trained in his father's shop. But the shop broke up in 1514, and the father moved to Isenheim; the two sons went to Basle, and worked there partly as painters, partly for publishers, and Hans, in 1515 or '16 came in contact with Erasmus. He also began painting portraits, the finest of them being the pair of *Jacob Meyer and his Wife*. Meyer was the Burgomaster of Basle, and he represented the rise of a

139 BURGKMAIR *St John the Evangelist on Patmos*, 1518

successful bourgeois merchant to high civic office in a University town. The drawing made for these portraits prove that right from the start Holbein developed his technique of working from drawings. In 1517 he left Basle, went to Lucerne, and may even have gone on to Italy; he was away two years, returned to become a citizen in 1520, and married – not very successfully on the evidence. In 1519 he painted Bonifazius Amerbach, a scholar, collector, friend of Erasmus, who became a great collector of Holbein's work, as was his son – perhaps the first example of one collector buying consistently one artist's work. The great Amerbach collection was bought in 1662 by the City of Basle – the first case of civic patronage of this kind. Possibly the Amerbach portrait could support the argument that he had been to Italy in the interval; it is warmer in tone, fuller in modelling than the Meyer pair. The superb *Dead Christ* of 1521 was perhaps inspired by Grünewald's Isenheim altar, and may originally have been the predella of a now lost altarpiece. It is utterly realist, grim, with no religious atmosphere to relieve its starkness, more the portrait of a dead hero than a dead Christ, and completely unItalian. The Solothurn *Madonna and Child with Saints* of 1522, the *Passion* altar of 1521-25, or the Oberried altarpiece of about 1520-21, of which only part survived the iconoclasm of the Reformation, could all be used to support the thesis of an Italian journey before 1520; but by now the traffic in engravings made it much easier for an artist to assimilate Italian ideas. In 1521 he was commissioned to paint decorations in the City Council Chamber – a commission obtained through Meyer. It consisted of colonnades with figures representing the stock examples of law-givers, prophets, virtues and the like, but long before the decoration was completed changed religious conditions made alterations in the content necessary, and the work was broken off in 1522-23 after Meyer was dismissed from his Burgomastership. Later, on one of his return visits to Basle in 1530, Holbein took it up again in a rather different style, but it was more probably failure in technique than neglect that caused the frescoes to decay, so that they were finally obliterated in 1827. Drawings for the frescoes exist, as they also do for house façades painted in Basle, which also display a very definite northern Italian character. During this period he was working continually for publishers, notably for

140 HOLBEIN *Madonna and Child, c.* 1525

Froben, who published both Erasmus, and Thomas More's 'Utopia'. He made the title page for the 1522 Luther New Testament, and designed the 'Dance of Death', 1523-6, and the 'Alphabet of Death', of 1524. Both these add the new bitterness of the Peasants' War to the medieval theme, and he varied the iconography of the Dance, by substituting the idea of Death striking unexpectedly at representatives of every human occupation and type. For political reasons the 'Dance of Death' was first published in Lyons in 1538, in Latin and French, and was so popular that it went through ten editions in twelve years.

By 1523 Holbein had established his reputation as a portrait painter with three portraits of Erasmus, who had now settled in

141 HOLBEIN
Wife and Children, c. 1530

Basle, and two of these were sent to England in 1524. The major
religious work of this period was again painted for Burgomaster
Meyer – the *Madonna and Child* with the Meyer family as donors,
which must, for religious reasons, have been finished before 1526,
when, in any case, Holbein left Basle (*Pl. 140*). This very fine work,
and the two portraits of *Magdalena Offenburg* (*Pl. 142*), one dated
1526, once more raise the question of an Italian journey, and it
seems inescapable that by this time he must, in fact, have gone at
least to north Italy, possibly after he was in Lyons in 1524. The portraits of Magdalena are very Raphaelesque in type, but the Meyer
Madonna and other portraits have a distinct air of Moretto, Lotto,
or Savoldo, influences which were less likely to have been transmitted by means of engravings.

In 1526 he made his first journey to England, travelling through
the Netherlands and visiting Matsys in Antwerp. He had letters of
introduction from Erasmus to More and to William Warham, Archbishop of Canterbury; he stayed eighteen months, and then returned
to Basle until 1532. He found that the religious troubles had become

42 HOLBEIN *Magdalena Offenburg as Venus*, 1526

worse, that pictures were now being torn from churches and burnt, and iconoclastic riots occurred. He worked again for publishers in Basle and Lyons, did some designs for stained glass (which survived as an art in Basle despite religious troubles, since it was a major local industry), endeavoured to continue the Council Chamber decorations, painted a few portraits, including the terrible one of the wife and children he was so soon to abandon – terrible because of a pitiless realism and a chillingly dispassionate observation almost without feeling (*Pl. 141*). Attempts were made by the council to retain him, a pension was offered, but Holbein, who had done well out of his English visit, was determined to go once civil war had broken out again in 1531. Possibly the *Noli me Tangere*, with its strange lighting and lurid colour, was painted about now, but in 1532 he turned his back for good on Basle and returned to London.

ENGLAND

When Holbein arrived in England in 1526, his letters of introduction from Erasmus secured him a welcome from the household of the most enlightened humanist in the land. It is possible that he did some work for the court, and the portraits of *Sir Henry* and *Lady Guildford* indicate a link with the court, since Sir Henry was Comp-

143 HOLBEIN *Sir John Godsalve, c.* 1528

144 HOLBEIN *Georg Gisze,* 1532

FAMILIA THOMÆ MORI ANGL: CANCELL:

Thomas Morus Æ.50. Alicia Thomæ Mori uxor Æ.57. Iohannes Morus pater Æ.76. Iohannes Morus Thomæ filius Æ.19. Anna Grisacria Iohannis Mori Sponsa Æ.15. Margareta Ropera Thomæ Mori filia Æ.22. Elisabeta Dancia Thomæ Mori filia Æ.21. Cæcilia Heroina Thomæ Mori filia Æ.20. Margareta Giga Clementis uxor Mori filiabus Condiscipula et cognata Æ.22. Henricus Patensonus Thomæ Mori morio Æ.40.

145 HOLBEIN *Thomas More and his Family.* Drawing, 1527

troller to the Household. But his real field was with More and his circle.

The group of the More family now exists only in copies, and in the drawing made by Holbein himself which was sent to Erasmus (*Pl. 145*). In 1529 Erasmus wrote to More about the pleasure he felt 'when the painter Holbein gave me the picture of your whole family, which is so completely successful that I should scarcely be able to see you better if I were with you'. This is by far the most elaborate of the humanist scholar-in-his-setting portraits, and as a composition is completely natural and yet very subtle in the way it preserves the family hierarchy. He also painted several versions of *Archbishop Warham*, clearly done from a drawing, so that he conti-

165

nued the method first worked out in the Meyer portraits. Two other important portraits date from this first visit: one of *Nicolas Kratzer*, Astronomer to Henry VIII, taking up the Erasmus type of scholar portraits, with a bravura display of still-life detail in the mathematical instruments surrounding him; and the double portrait of *Sir Thomas Godsalve and his son*, for the son was later connected with the Merchants of the Steelyard who became Holbein's chief patrons at the start of his second visit (*Pl. 143*).

When Holbein returned in 1532, More was at the point of falling from power, and during the next four years the painter found his market among the German merchants. The portrait of *Georg Gisze* (*Pl. 144*) of 1532 was the display sample which brought in custom, for it is a fantastic piece of bravura still-life painting, excelling even the Kratzer portrait. Until now, Henry VIII had paid no attention to the artist, but he seems suddenly to have realized after seeing the *Ambassadors* (*Pl. 146*), that Holbein was a painter who could put him on a par with Francis I. Royal patronage was continuous from 1536, beginning with the great dynastic family portrait of Henry VII and Elizabeth of York, and Henry VIII with Jane Seymour, lost in the fire at Whitehall in 1698. Part of the cartoon survives, and a poor copy gives an idea of what the original aimed at. The cartoon of *Henry VIII* (*Pl. 147*) served as the basis for the numerous portraits of the king, painted to be sent abroad, mostly accompanying marriage embassies, and the main idea behind Henry's patronage was not the encouragement of the arts for themselves, but as objects of court policy embodying and bolstering his dynastic claims. Holbein's technique of painting from drawings was strengthened by his practice as a court artist, but slowly his style became more linear, partly because of the demand for precise detail and partly because painting only from drawings leads to a decline in the atmospheric quality of colour and the sensitiveness of handling. The inclusion of legends and armorial bearings tends also to reduce the reality of the portrait and convert it into an effigy, yet he never loses sight of the character of his sitter. In his portrait of *Jane Seymour* he is merciless towards her narrow, pinched, hypocritical face, her mean, sharp eyes, her pursed mouth and hard thrusting chin; Cromwell's cruel, pig-like features are done full justice; and even his royal master's unamiable character

166

is not in any way glossed over by favourable posing or attempts at idealization.

His designs for Henry VIII's palace at Nonesuch suffer from his passion for detail, since it – as much as his patron's uneducated taste – led him into Certosa-like excesses of ornament. But these must have represented opportunities for the kind of large-scale work in which he had been thwarted in Basle, and which, equally, he had little scope for in England. He portrayed Henry as Solomon in one decoration at Whitehall, and a group of the *Presentation of*

the Charter to the Barber-Surgeons shows Henry so much larger than the other figures that it is clear that he is using the medieval iconography of religious painting for modern secular purposes. What this dispassionate realist, who portrayed his half-blind and sick wife with such unemotional exactness, made of a commission which required him to represent the gross and bloated king, whom he had already had to portray as Solomon, virtually in the guise of God surrounded by humble votaries gathered about him as lesser beings than he; what he made of a milieu in which this distortion of human and spiritual values could occur, is perhaps best understood from the hard, set, disillusioned gaze with which he portrayed himself. Even in his death he was cheated, for he died of plague in 1543, at the age of only forty-six. The tragedy of Holbein is that, as one of the great artists of his age, he found himself constrained by the

147 HOLBEIN *Henry VIII.*
Cartoon, 1537

148 HOLBEIN *Self-Portrait*.
Miniature, 1543

accidents of politics to work for patrons who had no use for any other form of art than portraiture; while this made of him one of the great portrait painters of all time, it was, nevertheless, a crippling limitation of his genius (*Pl. 148*).

If Holbein had a studio, then remarkably little trace of it remained after his death. The John Bettes who signed a *Portrait of an Unknown Man* (Tate Gallery) in 1545, may have been an assistant of his, but neither Guillim Scrots nor Gerlach Flicke could have been. Scrots (who used to be known as Stretes) came here from the Netherlands in 1545, and Flicke from Germany in 1547. Scrots is the finer artist, painting in a distinctly Italianate style with a good deal of Moretto in it; he is responsible for the series of distinguished portraits – possibly commemorative – of the *Earl of Surrey*, who was executed in the winter of 1546-47 (*Pl. 149*). They are all full-length portraits, and this form, invented in Germany, seems to have taken root in England more rapidly than it did elsewhere. Holbein's *Ambassadors* of 1533 is usually referred to as the first instance in England, but there is a life-sized, full-length, seated portrait of *Richard II*, which should be earlier than 1399, and even if it were a commemorative effigy would not be much later than the first decade of the fifteenth century. There is also the Holbein group of the More family, painted in 1527, which contained at least five standing figures besides the seated ones. Since the Nostell Priory copy is 8 × 13 feet, it seems reasonable to suggest that Holbein's original group must have been life-sized as well, and may in fact have been a cartoon, like the later dynastic group of Henry VII and VIII, and intended to become a wall decoration. This would explain why it is mentioned as a 'water-colour', and would also explain features like the perspective, the furniture, the hangings, the clock on the wall, and the view through the open door. It would

in fact be an extension into portraiture of the Council Room decorations, or the house-façade paintings in Basle.

During Mary's reign, the most considerable foreign artist to
appear, somewhat fleetingly, on the English scene was Anthonis
Mor, a Netherlandish court portrait painter much employed by
Philip of Spain and the Hapsburg courts in Flanders. Mor, or Moro,
to give his name its common Italianate form, was in England in
1554 to paint a marriage portrait of Mary for Philip II, and his
cold, Bronzino-like type of professional face painting continued the
realist and detached tradition of Holbein, merely adding a little more
amplitude to the setting, as befitted the mid-century and an artist
who knew at first hand what portraits were like in Rome, Florence
and Venice (*Pl. 150*).

The most interesting painter working continuously in England
after Holbein was Hans Eworth, the Master of the HE monogram.
He was an Antwerp man, who came here after 1540 and died about
1574. His portraits, all on panel, have the objectivity of Holbein,

149 SCROTS *Earl of Surrey*,
1546 or later

150 MOR *Queen Mary*, 1554   151 EWORTH *Lady Dacre*, 1540

but with slightly more humanity (*Pl. 151*); he also painted allegorical subjects – if the identification of the slightly differently shaped HE monogram on them is right. He is an artist with a strong sense of pattern and immense ability in detail, but except for the rather clumsy adulatory allegories on the glory of Elizabeth, which would reflect the world of his employment as a court masque designer, there is no repercussion in England of trends in Fontainebleau or in Italy. Elizabeth's favourite painter, with a monopoly in her portraits secured by a patent, was Nicholas Hilliard. He is the first native artist of whom anything like a life history or a proper corpus of works can be established; he was a goldsmith, born in 1547, who painted miniatures as part of his jeweller's art, and was doing so from about 1560, his first portrait of Elizabeth being dated 1570. His 'Portraits in littel' are as jewel-like as their settings, and their style is explained in his treatise 'The Arte of Limning' written in 1600, which echoed his conversations with the Queen in their agreement that portraits were '...best in plain lines and without shadowing'. His transparent flesh tints, and the perfection of his treatment of forms

152 OLIVER
Richard Sackville,
Earl of Dorset, 1616

in terms of pure light, have almost nothing in common with Holbein, Eworth or Mor. Hilliard achieved something that they never attempted: a degree of idealization, of seeing the best in a sitter, totally alien to their dispassionate, and sometimes unfriendly pursuit of an exact likeness. A contemporary appreciation of his art is to be found in one of Donne's poems of, probably, 1597: '...a hand, or eye

153   HILLIARD
Young Man amid Roses, c. 1590

By Hilliard drawne, is worth an history By a worse painter made',
and Haydocke, in his 'Tracte Containinge The Artes of curious
Paintinge', published in 1598, compared him to '...the milde spirit
of the late worldes-wonder Raphael Urbine'. By 1600 he was in
financial difficulties, perhaps because his chief pupil Isaac Oliver was
able to rival him technically, while having a much more up-to-date

style, with overtones of French and Italian painting. Oliver was French by origin, since he had come to England in 1568 as the child of Huguenot refugee parents. He visited Venice in 1596, and had ambitions towards grander forms than portrait miniatures; he wanted to extend painting 'in littel' to history painting, and is recorded as making fine copies in drawing after Parmigianino. He never feared shadows in his faces, and developed the backgrounds of his miniatures in great depth, with rich details of Turkey carpets, embroidered hangings, and feathered helmets. He often painted full-length figures, which are less common in Hilliard's works, where the flamboyant figure of the *Earl of Cumberland* of about 1590, or the exquisite Mannerist elegance of the *Young Man amid Roses* (*Pl. 153*), also about 1590, is the more outstanding for being unusual. Oliver's miniatures are often very rich in colour and very high in key: the *Earl of Dorset* (*Pl. 152*), for instance wears embroidered blue stockings and short-hose, and stands in front of rich blue curtains, and red velvet table cloth. After Elizabeth's death in 1603, Hilliard was confirmed by James I in all his official patents, but Oliver had the greater popularity at court, where Hilliard's poetry and imagery was somewhat old-fashioned. Oliver died first, in 1617, and Hilliard, eighteen months later in 1619.

The great art form of the sixteenth century in England was not painting – sculpture existed only as funerary monuments, the greatest of which were the Tudor tombs in Henry VII's Chapel by the Italian Torrigiano – but architecture, for this was an art which combined pride of possession and display in land, with the deep need of a new aristocracy and landed class, which had acquired wealth and property as a result of Henry VIII's distribution of confiscated monastic lands, to put down roots in their new possessions. Hence the evolution from the convenient but asymmetrical and untidy forms of the medieval manor to the grand, many-storeyed, many-windowed mansion, designed on a central axis and frequently based on plans derived from Serlio and Palladio, and built of stone. Sometimes the inspiration was French, as it was with the first Somerset House, in the Stand, built about 1549 and later demolished, but generally it was the kind of classical Italy that inspired John Shute, the writer of the first book on architecture in English, and the first Englishman to describe himself as an 'architect' on the title page of his 'The First and Chief Groundes of Architecture', of 1563. Shute had been sent by his patron, the Duke of Northumberland, to Italy about 1550, but his early death in 1563 left little but the influence of his well-illustrated volume. This is a passably good imitation of an Italian textbook, and shows not only that he knew how to improve on Serlio, but that he also knew such classics as Fra Giocondo's illustrated edition of Vitruvius of 1551, Alberti's treatise in its earliest illustrated form, published in Florence in 1550, and Barbaro's edition of Vitruvius, published in 1556 with Palladio's illustrations. Vignola's 'Regole delli Cinque Ordini...' of 1562, and Palladio's 'Quattro Libri dell'Architettura' of 1570, came too late to affect Shute. There were also Flemish and German architectural books, such as those by Hans Blum of 1550, Vredeman de Vries from 1562 onwards, Wendel Dietterlin from 1593, but these had little practical influence except occasionally as models for decorative details. Another stimulus to the rising interest in architecture, theoretical as well as practical, can be found in the engraved title pages of books printed on Italian presses, since these often contributed indirectly to the ever-widening dissemination of classical architectural forms.

Many great houses of the Elizabethan age display a curious mixture of Italianate detail with the surviving habits of Perpendicular Gothic, in the combination of classical orders with the huge areas of glass in a framework of rectilinear mullions and transoms. Kirby in Northamptonshire, begun in 1570 and now a ruin, is the first instance in England of a giant order. The house is built around a central courtyard; the entrance wing has an arcaded loggia facing on to the court and the piers of this loggia are faced with a giant order of pilasters, the four outer ones fluted and the central pair carved with a rich candelabra ornament running up to their very fanciful capitals. On the other side of the court, the main living quarters consist, on one side, of the great hall rising through the entire height of the building, and on the other of living rooms in two storeys. The entrance, in the centre, also serves as the screens passage of the hall. Kirby was probably built by Thomas Thorpe, the father of the John Thorpe who laid the first stone of Kirby when he was a child of six, and who became, at the beginning of the next century, an important architect and surveyor.

Queen Elizabeth's minister William Cecil, who began Burghley, near Stamford, in the 1550s, not only finished the house on a huge scale between 1572 and 1587; he also built an even more grandiose mansion for one of his sons at Theobalds in Hertfordshire. Theobalds had five courtyards, with great turretted corner blocks linked by lower wings borne on arcaded loggias, but its splendour vanished for ever in 1650, and its influence can only be sensed in its contemporaries and in successors such as nearby Hatfield, also built by the Cecils. Burghley begins traditionally enough with an old-fashioned centrepiece in the middle of the entrance front – a tower gateway with projecting windows compressed between tall turrets. In the great arcaded courtyard, however, the main feature is a second huge tower, built up of arches flanked by niches with columns on either side, rising in a sequence of orders to the enormous square clock face supported by heraldic lions and crowned by a tall pyramidal steeple. Cecil imported architectural books to help him with his vast building projects: he had Philibert de l'Orme's 'Nouvelles Inventions Pour Bien Bastir...', first published in 1561, sent from Paris, and he probably also knew Philibert's other works, the 'Premier Tome de l'Architecture' of 1567, and the invaluable books by du Cerceau – the 'Architectura' of 1559, and the first and second volumes of his ' des plus excellents Bastiments de France', which first appeared in 1574. The character of the clock tower at Burghley suggests an attempt to consider a building not merely as an assemblage of decorative features applied erratically to the outside of a traditional structure, but as blocks of masonry arranged so as to create a structure coherent and valid in itself, much as Philibert had done in the gateway, chapel, and frontispiece of Anet, or Bullant had done at Écouen in the 1550s, where one of the main entrances, known from an engraving by du Cerceau, closely recalls the Burghley clock tower.

Serlio's books on architecture had a considerable effect on the best of the late sixteenth-century architects, Robert Smythson, who was described as an architect on his tomb in 1614. Smythson was born about 1536, and first appears as one of the men working on Longleat, building for the third time under the exigent eye of its owner, Sir John Thynne, after the fire that gutted it in 1567. Smythson did not design the house, which in the main was rebuilt on the foundations and lower courses of the previous structure, but from 1572 onwards he was largely responsible for recladding it with its present façades – a rhythmical arrangement of salient and retreating bays, three storeys high, articulated in a rising sequence of Doric, Ionic and Corinthian orders. Longleat is now not much more than a shell since its symmetrical exterior masks the early nineteenth-century alterations to its original four courtyards, two of which were combined into one, and the thorough Victorian remodelling of the interior. But from the outside the pattern of light and dark made by the huge windows in the golden stone is as rhythmic as the alternation of bays and the skilful use of the orders to divide the storeys. The house is crowned by a balustrade, now bearing later statuary, and by elaborate carved gables over the bay windows. Small domed turrets, many of them belonging to the earlier stages of the house, pierce the flat roofline, and, together with the numerous decorative chimneys, give an impression similar to that made, on a far more lavish scale, by Chambord, from which the device of the little turret rooms designed to serve as a kind of summertime arbour, was probably derived (*Pl. 154*).

After Longleat, virtually finished by 1580, the year Thynne died, Smythson began Wollaton, a house at once more spectacular and less coherent than Longleat (*Pl. 155*). The main body of Wollaton is symmetrical about a central axis, just as Longleat is on the outside, but at Wollaton there is no interior courtyard and a great hall towers above the surrounding structure, imparting a deliberately medieval air to the house. It looks at first sight as if an older hall had been encased in a later rebuilding, since the windows of the hall are two-light, round-headed openings in contrast to the huge rectilinear windows of the outer parts of the house, and the corners of the hall are trimmed with projecting watch-towers, decorative and totally belying their apparent function. There is more decoration, too, in the little niches and the strap-work pediments over the massive towers that form the corner blocks. In fact, Smythson derived the plan from Serlio, and he found in de Vries patterns for the rich detailing of the cartouches, the strap-work of the pediments, and the carving on the hall screen.

Between 1590 and 1595 Smythson built Hardwick Hall for the celebrated Bess of Hardwick, the widow of the Earl of Shrewsbury

154 SMYTHSON Longleat, 1572-80

155 SMYTHSON Wollaton Hall, 1580-88

156 Attributed to SMYTHSON, Hardwick Hall, 1590-97

for whom he had built the now destroyed Worksop Manor. In plan, Hardwick is almost as symmetrical inside, about its central great hall, as it is on the outside, and the great hall, rising through the two lower storeys provides for communication between the two halves of the house and also serves as a centrally placed main entrance leading from the colonnaded loggia. 'Hardwick Hall, more glass than wall' the saying goes, and the gigantic rectilinear windows, in their advancing and retreating bays and towers, create a marvellous effect of movement, and of the mass of the house being yet more void than solid. It is one of the characteristics of these huge areas of window that they permitted considerable variation in the height of the rooms behind them, so that the floor levels of what appear to be clearly defined storeys are by no means all on the same plane. This means that sometimes windows came in awkward places – low down or very high up – inside the rooms, though preserving the regular pattern on the outside, and it involved a

179

maze of small staircases within the structure. This, again, was a feature largely eliminated in the seventeenth century, when smaller windows and, on the whole, more compact houses tended to greater evenness of room height. Hardwick is typical of this kind of infinitely varied room design, for the great hall runs through two floors, and the long gallery also runs through two floors, but not the same two, and in the tower blocks the room heights vary as between one block and another (*Pl. 156*).

All these great Elizabethan houses mark the change, social as much as architectural, in the nature of the great hall, for instead of being the central feature of a house, as it had been in the fifteenth century, its role now was purely a show one. It was still included for use on grand occasions, as at Hatfield (1607-12), but the family now inhabited private apartments instead of presiding over the communal life which made sense of the old type of great hall. It is one of the instances of an architectural form long outliving the purpose for which it was originally designed, for it persisted until in the seventeenth century it finally became no more than an entrance vestibule, as at Charlton, Blackheath (1607), and the neighbouring Queen's House, Greenwich (begun in 1616). It was inevitable that the staircase well should also merge with it, so that it becomes a central area of communication: a connecting unit rather than a focal point.

The Queen's House, which developed this new concept of the central hall, also marked the end of the last splendid phase of the 'prodigy' house, and with Inigo Jones English architecture joined the main current of Renaissance inspiration. It is curious to think that the years which saw the final burst of the Perpendicular in the completion of Henry VII's chapel at Westminster Abbey, finished about 1520, are the years in which Michelangelo was designing the architecture of the Medici Chapel – already the second stage of Renaissance architecture in Italy; that Longleat and the Gesù are contemporary; and that when Hardwick Hall was begun Palladio had already been dead for some ten years. When Inigo Jones completed the Banqueting House in Whitehall in 1622, a totally new era had already opened in the arts of Western Europe.

CHAPTER FIVE

The Renaissance in Spain

Three factors govern the development of the arts in Spain during the sixteenth century: the centralization of power in the monarchy under Ferdinand and Isabella, confirmed under Charles V, which diminished the nobility and reduced the bourgeoisie to an insignificant status; the continual wars against the Moors and then the Turks, and the involvement of Spain in Italian, German and Netherlandish affairs through the vast inheritance of Charles V and his succession to the Empire in 1519; the identification of the crown with the Church. Virtually the only patronage was religious patronage; decoration, as it was understood in the north and in Italy found almost no scope, except in a religious context. Some Spanish artists worked in Italy, notably Pedro Berruguete, a Castilian who may have been in Urbino in the late fifteenth century, and Alonso Berruguete, who was in Italy from 1504-17, who received letters of introduction from Michelangelo to friends in Florence in 1508, and who participated in the general development of Mannerism there, but without being anything more than a follower of new trends. After his return to Spain, he developed into one of the major sculptors of his day, and was perhaps the most considerable artist working in Spain before the arrival of El Greco. Under Isabella a great deal of Flemish painting had been imported, chiefly for the royal collection; Charles V imported Italian artists to work on the decoration of the Escorial; and then Philip II became possibly the largest single buyer of Titian's works. Where Renaissance motives crept in, it was in a watered-down yet exaggerated form, provincial and mixed with Flemish influences, as in the work of Juan de Juanes. Anthonis Mor – or Antonio Moro – was the most prolific portraitist of the mid-century, with a practice which took him into all the Hapsburg courts of Europe, and sent him travelling from Rome to London.

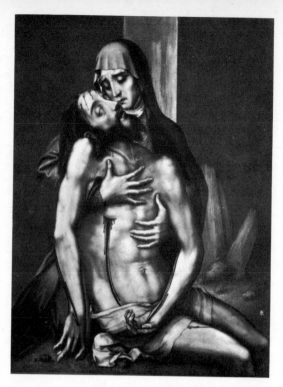

His successor was Sánchez Coello, a painter who trained in Portugal, where he executed some religious works, before he became Court Painter to Philip II in 1557. His style is the rigid, formal one evolved by Mor for the representation of state personages in icons to be distributed among all the Hapsburg connections of Europe, but it is more summary, with less sensitive modelling even though he does occasionally betray the influence of Titian.

Two men express the Spanish ideal fully: Luis Morales and El Greco. Morales is documented from 1547 in Badajoz, where he spent most of his life, dying there in 1586. He received some training from a Dutchman, but his style was based principally on Flemish Italianate painters who derived largely from Leonardo and his Milanese followers, and who transmitted to him a predilection for soft forms melting into dark shadows, and on Italian Mannerists such as Rosso, as well as Michelangelo and Sebastiano del Piombo, whom he could have known from engravings. Works by Sebastiano were in Spain: a *Deposition* at Úbeda in Andalusia, depends upon a

Michelangelo drawing, and a *Christ carrying the Cross*, reminiscent of the Giorgione one, was painted about 1537 for a Conde de Cifuentes who lived in Toledo. It was in Spain until looted by Marshal Soult during the Napoleonic campaigns. There were also two works in the Spanish royal collection: a *Christ carrying the Cross*, of about 1525-27, and a *Christ in Limbo*, of about 1528-30: if Morales had ever seen a Sebastiano at all, and the iconography of some of his works suggests that he did, then the two in the royal collection could have been seen about 1564, since he is believed to have worked for Philip II in Madrid then. All his pictures are of religious subjects, and he specialized in rather highly-wrought *Depositions* and *Pietàs*, (*Pl. 157*), and also in very tender *Madonna and Child* groups; in fact, his tormented imagery and vision gained for him the nickname of 'El Divino'. It can be argued that since neither he nor El Greco ever had anything more than local popularity, and that neither was much patronized by Philip II, the 'Spanishness' of their vision is more convincing to foreigners than an actual fact. Spanish taste tended much more to the harsh realism of Navarrete ('El Mudo' – 'The Dumb'), whose *Martyrdom of St Lawrence* of 1579 in the Escorial is a forerunner of the sombre Caravaggism of the next century, and a fitting prelude to Ribera and Velazquez. Yet the intense

159 EL GRECO *El Espolio,* 1577-79

religious emotion of Morales and El Greco fits in with the religious literary climate of St Ignatius Loyola, St Theresa of Avila, and St John of the Cross.

El Greco was born in Crete in 1541, and possibly received some training in the late – but still surviving – Byzantine tradition of icon painting before he arrived in Venice in his early twenties. There are very few references to his Italian years, but a mention of him in a letter from the miniaturist Giulio Clovio to Cardinal Farnese in 1570 speaks of him as a young Cretan, a pupil of Titian, who had arrived in Rome. There is also a curious account of him in Mancini's 'Considerazioni sulla Pittura', which the writer continued adding to until his death in 1630: he says that El Greco was working in Rome in the time of Pius V (1566-72), that he had been with Titian, and was a successful painter who came to Rome when the city lacked artists of spontaneity and decisiveness of style. He had so great a conceit of himself that when Pius proposed to cover

184

the nudes in Michelangelo's *Last Judgement*, El Greco offered, if it were demolished, to paint another as good, and chaste and decorous in addition. This caused such great resentment that he was forced to retire to Spain, but since he arrived uninvited, he had to compete with Pellegrino Tibaldi, Federico Zuccaro, and several Flemings who had precedence at court through their work and their intrigues. 'So he left the court and retired to ... where he died very old and forgotten.' Now Mancini is an unreliable authority, but there are sufficient things right in this note to make the rest credible. El Greco is recorded as being anti-Michelangelo, since he shocked Pacheco, Velazquez's teacher, by saying that Michelangelo 'was a good man, but could not paint'; he was a pupil of Titian; he did make one bid for court patronage in Madrid, and failed; he arrived in Rome in 1570, and Pius lived until 1572.

The connection between El Greco and Titian is sometimes discounted in favour of one with Tintoretto instead. Not only is his work deeply influenced by Titian, in style, in technique, with

figures borrowed from him; but there is no such close connection between El Greco and Tintoretto. If one equates the early style of Tintoretto with the arrival of Mannerism in Venice, one must also remember that elongated figures, startling contrasts of colour and the use of acid and sharp colours, the placing of the main incident deep into the picture space, were all features of central Italian Mannerism long before they appear in Tintoretto, and were known by the usual currents. The extravagant emotionalism, the wonderful use of violent contrasts of colour, and the force of the linear patterns associated with Tintoretto were developed far more after El Greco had gone to Spain than before. They derive, in many ways, from common sources: both used Byzantine ideas – El Greco because his earliest training penetrated his adopted style and his work came to be a synthesis of both; Tintoretto because as he grew older the force and eloquence of Byzantine models in Venice accorded with the direction his style was taking. But both also used central Italian Mannerism as a well from which they drew what they needed for their own personal expression. Their independence of each other is vouched for by the fact that El Greco also used ideas derived from Bassano and Veronese. Even Titian himself in the late 1560s was moving towards the greater expressiveness which is the reflection of Mannerism in his work.

The early *Christ and the Money Changers* of about 1572-4 is only partly full of the things El Greco had seen in Venice during the last years; it must have been painted in Rome, for the architecture is that of a basilica of an entirely Roman type, while the architectural background of some of his earlier pictures is derived from the plates of theatrical settings in Serlio. It has also four portraits in the foreground: Titian, his master, and Michelangelo, Giulio Clovio, his friend and protector in Rome, and Raphael (*Pl. 158*). The composition is very odd, but the powerful oblique of the architecture is similar to that in both pictures of the *Healing of the Blind Man* (Dresden and Parma), and to the Washington version of the *Money Changers*, which is rather earlier. The curious shapes of the floor and its changes in level, the tightly packed mass of figures driven to one side, the opulent semi-nude women, the vigorous torsos of the young men, and, above all, the colour, all point to experiments and borrowings, but also to a new vision. The odd device of the four mentors is patently derived from Salviati's *Visitation* of 1538 in S. Giovanni Decollato in Rome, and similar effects in the architectural setting and attendant figures occur there too. His early portraits – for instance, the one of Clovio in Naples, or of Giovanni Battista Porto in Copenhagen – depend not so much on Titian as on Bassano, who is probably also the inspiration for his wonderful candlelight pictures such as the *Boy blowing on a Brand* (Naples, and elsewhere). One very grand portrait of Vincentio Anastagi, later a Governor of Malta, painted about 1575-6, suggests memories of Titian's state portraits, or of Veronese's *Paolo Guarienti* in Verona. This was the tradition which Caravaggio later used for *Alof de Vignacourt*, and which was valid for Rubens and Van Dyck. By this time he had developed a vigorous and forceful style, which fits in with Mancini's opinion that no Roman artist had the spontaneity and firmness of his style.

161 EL GRECO *Martyrdom of St Maurice and the Theban Legion*, 1580-84

162 EL GRECO *Cardinal Guevara, c.* 1600

EL GRECO *Burial of Count Orgaz,* 1586

That he visited the north again at the end of his stay in Rome is suggested by his copy of Correggio's *Nativity*, '*La Notte*' in Parma, and also because immediately after his arrival in Spain his colour has a much more vibrant, singing quality than during the years in Rome, when he was gradually subdued, possibly by the influence of Michelangelo.

The commission for the high altar and a pair of side altars for S. Domingo el Antiguo in Toledo was given in 1577, and from a comment made by El Greco during the lawsuit over the payment for the *Espolio* (*Pls. 159, 160*), he apparently came to Toledo to paint them; the inference is that he went first to Madrid where he sought patronage unsuccessfully. All but two of the pictures on the high altar were later sold off and dispersed; the other altars remain in the church. The high altar consisted of an *Assumption* (Chicago), a *Trinity* (Prado), and four saints, of which two remain. The side altars contain a *Nativity* and a *Resurrection*. The derivation of the *Trinity* from Dürer's print of 1511 is perfectly obvious, yet the design has a coherence which does not immediately drive one into looking for prototypes. Above all, the scale is astonishing; so far as is known, El Greco had never before painted anything larger than about five feet wide, but this is nearly ten feet high, and nowhere is there any difficulty with the scale. The same applies even more to the *Assumption*, which is over sixteen feet high. Like all other *Assumptions* of the late sixteenth and seventeenth centuries, it is borrowed from Titian, though the changes are in the direction of a more Mannerist approach. The composition is more open than Titian's, and the emotion, though quieter, is more in keeping with Counter-Reformation ideas of contemplation of a mystery rather than excited witnessing of a miracle. In the *Resurrection* altar the reminiscences are strongly of the circular movement of the Cappella Paolina, with figures drawn from Pontormo and Parmigianino, and the *Nativity* is a variation on Correggio's theme. Immediately after the S. Domingo altars, the *Espolio* was commissioned for the cathedral sacristy. Many versions were later made and the studio produced numerous copies. The picture was nearly refused by the authorities, and El Greco sued them for his fee. The objections appear at first sight to be usual ones of the visually uneducated – the figure of Christ was not dominant, heads of thieves and executioners are higher than His, the Holy Women are included, whereas the text says they watched from afar – but this is far more the result of a literal application of Counter-Reformation rules on propriety and decorum in pictures. Fortunately, the assessors declared that the picture was beyond price. With the exception of portraits, El Greco worked almost exclusively for the church, which was a powerful and insatiable patron; Toledo was the Holy City of Spain and contained nearly a thousand religious houses and churches, being more pious, more exclusively given over to religion than Rome itself. It had industries – it was famous for swords, jewellery, ceramics, weaving – and at the beginning of El Greco's residence was busy and prosperous, but at the time of his death whole districts were abandoned and grass grew in the streets.

The *Dream of Philip* (Escorial, Chapter House; sketch in the National Gallery, London) was painted for Philip II about 1579, and must be seen against the background of Titian's *La Gloria*, which is an allegory of salvation, with Charles V, Philip's father, as the chief penitent intercessor; in the *Dream*, which is an allegory of the Holy League against the Infidel, Philip is granted a vision of a salvation that can only be obtained by uniting Christendom against heresy, which is being destroyed in the mouth of Hell immediately behind him. Eventually, El Greco received an important commission in 1580 for a *Martyrdom of St Maurice and the Theban Legion*, destined for the chapel of the Escorial (*Pl. 161*). He delivered it in 1584, and Philip immediately rejected it. The King's secretary, Siguenza, wrote: 'The picture does not please His Majesty, and that is no wonder, for it pleases few, although it is said that there is much art in it and its author understands much, for there are excellent things of his to be seen.' Philip only loved one thing besides religion, and that was art; but it was the deep, rich, sonorous, passionate art of Titian that he loved, full of wonderful harmonies of form and sensibilities of colour, and conforming still to the ideas current in the High Renaissance. The *St Maurice* (now in the Escorial Sacristy) reflects the troubled art of Pontormo and the famous cartoon by Perino del Vaga (*Pl. 25*) which so excited Florence in 1523. It has all the dispersion of effects, the flaring, startling colour, the odd long shots into tight groups of figures in the far distance, that characterize Mannerist works, and betoken a dark cast of mind, an

anxious questing for new solutions to old problems. The trouble, basically, was that El Greco's art reflected a world which Philip refused to recognize. He turned from the one artist who could have solved all his problems of patronage, all the difficulties over the decoration of the Escorial which drove him to import inferior Italian art and artists, because he could not accept that the tension and the strain of El Greco's imagery was the true reflection of the world he had contributed so much to create about him.

In 1586 El Greco completed the *Burial of Count Orgaz*, the miracle of the faithful and charitable knight buried by Sts Augustine and Stephen before a crowd of mourners (*Pl. 163*). Above the earthly apotheosis is the heavenly one, to which the angel bears the soul of the dead man to judgemant and mercy. Not only does heaven lie over earth like a cloud, but like a curtain the vault of heaven is drawn aside to show the reward of piety. The heavenly part is not more visionary than the scene on earth: only differently so. The colour changes are more intense, more luminous, more strident, more of the bitter contrasts of blue and violet, and yellow and a shrill green. The forms are now beginning to transcend those of Italian Mannerism by accentuating the elongation of limbs, by giving them that curious nerve-drawn quality, and the strange feeling that the drapery they inhabit lives a life of its own with its own range of movement. There is also a certain return to Rosso and Pontormo, made vivid by the accidents of background. Both the Italians had experienced the terrors of war; in these years, until 1609, when the tragedy was virtually over in its immediate physical impact, El Greco was witnessing the expulsion of the Jews and the Moriscos. In 1585, the year before he began the *Orgaz*, he moved into a newly vacant twenty-four roomed palace in the old Jewish quarter of Toledo; when he died there in 1614, his worldly possessions could have been put in a good sized trunk and his debts pursued him from the grave through the life of his spendthrift son. The Toledo he loved, and which recurs so often as a background in his pictures – in the *St Martin* and the *St Joseph* both of 1597, in the *Laocoon* of about 1606, in the two views of Toledo of about 1605-9, in the two late *Crucifixions* – dwindled in these years and died, just as the dead craftsmen rotted on the beaches or, driven into the sea, perished in overcrowded boats that no one knew where to go in, or were captured by Barbary pirates and enslaved. Grass grew in the streets, the old prosperity of the steel workshops was gone, while bright Inca gold flowed in from the New World to destroy its own value by its profusion, and the only refuge from ruin was to seek a State sinecure so as to share in the gold that made trade impossible and work unnecessary, or to enter the religious houses that promised security amid the desolation.

The spiritual background of El Greco is in the atmosphere of the Spiritual Exercises of the Jesuits. If one compares his rendering of a scene with earlier versions he will never be found to linger over a casual assortment of bystanders; the crowd is strictly limited to the people who really matter – to the heart of the meaning. This is not merely the result of post-Tridentine precept, for Rubens's great religious pictures could never be placed outside the range of Tridentine art, yet they are never so limited in their means. The Spiritual Exercises suggest to the devout an imaginary presence at the event, seen in its simplest form and in its basic meaning. There is no evidence that El Greco practised the Exercises, as Bernini and Rubens did, but much in El Greco suggests that he knew and understood them, since one of the objects of the Exercises was to increase perception of spiritual states, and to promote the visionary and imaginative responses of the executant. Another factor was St John of the Cross. He lived in Toledo, where he was imprisoned by his enraged brethren who resented his attempts to reform his Order. Many of his poems seem to have welled out of him during his imprisonment and it is accepted that El Greco knew him. Many of St John's poems have the same intense, flickering, flame-like quality as El Greco's paintings, and in both the poet and the painter mystical experience is never destructive of form, but tends to heighten it and give it acute clarity of expression. But this intensity of feeling can be paralleled in pictures where immediate religious experience is out of the question. The portrait of *Cardinal Guevara* of c. 1600 – the Chief Inquisitor – is an instance of this heightening of perception and of the uncanny selection of just that facet of expression which will most tellingly evoke the awful power and character of the sitter and his office. The Cardinal is dressed in a wonderful pale purple with a froth of cool lace echoing his grey beard and his pallid face, so that the effect is one of frigid majesty (*Pl. 162*).

165 EL GRECO *View of Toledo*, 1595/1600

Even to the end of his life the forms of Italian Mannerism continued to inspire him. The *Pietà* in the Niarchos Collection of about 1580 should be compared with Titian's *Deposition* in the Prado, and Pontormo's S. Felicità *Deposition*, and then referred back to the ever-present memory of the Michelangelo *Pietà* to see how lasting were these influences, and in the same way, the very late *Visitation* (Dumbarton Oaks) harks back to Pontormo's *Visitation* at Carmignano, not only in the way the figures, seen partly from below, are related to each other, but also in the relation of the figures to their architectural setting.

During all these years he had produced a stream of copies and versions of the Toledo *Espolio*. Over the years, small changes crept in, always to heighten emotional impact and tension.

Through thy submitting all, to blows
Thy face, thy clothes to spoil, thy fame to scorn,
All ways, which rage or justice knows
And by which thou could'st show that thou wast born;
And through thy gallant humbleness
Which thou in death did'st show
Dying before thy soul they could express,
Deliver us from death by dying so
To this world, ere this world do bid us go.

Donne never knew the work he so perfectly describes, and the painter was separated from the poet not only by language but by faith. It is the expression of the age.

His last works prompt the suspicion that the last years before his death in 1614 were increasingly sad ones. The faithful contemplate the punishment of sin, and behind lies Toledo, the Holy City, yet the sky is rent with storms and the light is lurid and frightening. The lovely view of Toledo painted about 1609, with the city basking in the glory of heavenly protection, its vast Lamasseries spread out over the hill and spilling beyond the walls in piety and pride, bright, luminous and clear, gives place to the Toledo painted probably a year or two later, with the dark and terrible storms behind the Laocoon making it glow luridly in the flicker of unseen lightning (*Pl. 165*). Nothing is less truly Spanish than El Greco's art, for it was the culmination of Italian Mannerism. Morales in this sense was more truly Spanish, for his visions are pathetic without ecstasy, and his blend of Gothic emotion and harsh intensity of fact is more evocative of the Spanish mind than El Greco's more intuitive sensibility.

With a few notable exceptions, the end of the century saw a general decline of inspiration, and the 1570s was a decade of deaths. Eleven of the artists mentioned in these pages died in that decade. The exceptions were Venice, where Tintoretto continued to produce with an undiminished vigour until his death in 1594, and Florence, where Giovanni da Bologna worked into the early years of the next century, though Florentine painting was far below the level attained in sculpture. In Rome the architecture of Giacomo della Porta continued to be competent, though unimaginative and pedestrian. The main painters of the end of the century were feeble Mannerists, like the brothers Taddeo and Federico Zuccaro. Taddeo, who died in 1566, painted turgid frescoes in the Vatican, and decorated the Villa at Caprarola for the Farnese with complicated and eulogistic fresco cycles, which were completed after his death by his brother Federico, who lived until 1609. Federico travelled widely, was in Antwerp and France in 1574, and even came on to England, where he left behind a reputation for having painted Queen Elizabeth which furnishes half the country houses of England with lifeless effigies of very dissimilar doll-like creatures decked out in the most extravagant clothes and jewels. His only portrait of the queen with any claim to authenticity is the one in Siena, and even this is contested. He finished the frescoes in the dome of Florence cathedral which Vasari's death had prevented him from completing, and found when he went to Spain in 1585 that Philip II was still only interested in Titian's kind of art. In 1593 he established in his own house in Rome an Academy of which he became the first head in 1598, and this house itself is an extraordinary Mannerist conceit, since the doors and windows are fashioned like giant's faces. During his last years he concentrated on theories of art, and in particular on theories of ideal beauty and design. His bloodless and lifeless painting is the best commentary possible on the kind of art which he sought to encourage (*Pl. 167*).

The only other artist of repute who had a similarly peripatetic career, was Pellegrino Tibaldi, whose energy of style and determined use of violent perspective are based on a desire to push the ideas of Michelangelo to their furthest limit. He also blended the influence of Parmigianino and Niccolo dell'Abbate with Michelangelo, to produce colourful and fantastic decorations, like those, for instance, in Bologna in what is now the University (*Pl. 166*). He worked in Milan as an architect, in association with St Charles Borromeo, the Archbishop, building among other churches S. Fedele in a typical Counter-Reformation style. He was in Spain as well, from 1587 onwards, and there supervised the building and decoration of the Escorial, for which he painted forty-six frescoes in the cloisters. In 1596, he returned, noble and rich, to Milan, where he died in the same year. Of his energy and versatility there is no doubt, and many of his ceilings are astonishingly daring and inventive. The influence of Pellegrino on the Carracci in Bologna was important for the development of their decorative style, yet like Zuccaro he is a man very

167 FEDERICO ZUCCARO
Allegory of Design

much at the end of a tradition, at a moment of pause before new forms and ideas revivified the arts in the seventeenth century.

Largely, this dying fall is one of the accidents of history. The three main events of the century were the Reformation, the Sack of Rome, and the Council of Trent, and the third was the outcome of the other two. The Council, called to restate the articles of belief of the Catholic Church in the face of the Reformation, to reform abuses within the Church, and to unify the liturgy, also laid down certain rules affecting the arts, particularly in religious painting. It opened in 1545, and closed finally in 1563, and the decrees which affect the arts were promulgated in 1563. It was after the Council's ruling on decorum in religious paintings that Pius V had many of the figures in Michelangelo's *Last Judgement* furnished with loin-cloths. On the whole, the arts benefited from the decrees, after the first wave of uncertainties, though these naturally affected the development of late Mannerist art. Ultimately it was the renewal of confidence and rise of fervour and strength in faith that led to the great upsurge in the arts that characterizes the Baroque.

199

166 TIBALDI Ceiling decoration in the Palazzo Poggi, Bologna, begun 1553

Selected Bibliography

This is a brief list of the major books, mostly in English. All periodical literature has been excluded, and only a selection of monographs on the major artists is given.

Sources

By far the most important Italian source for the period is VASARI's *Vite* (1550 and, much enlarged, 1568): there is a full translation in 10 vols. by G. du C. de Vere, London, 1912-15, but the best English version of the most important *Lives* is by George Bull, Penguin Classics, London, 1965. The standard Italian edition is that edited by G. Milanesi, 9 vols., Florence, 1878-85, but there is an excellent modern edition published by the Club del Libro, 8 vols., Milan 1962-66. A national edition is in preparation: so far only two volumes (Florence, 1966, 1967) have appeared. For the Netherlands, the most important source is KAREL VAN MANDER's collection of *Lives*, published in Alkmaar in 1604, of which French (Paris, 1884) and English (New York, 1936) editions exist; but van Mander's work is in no way comparable with Vasari's.

A selection of translated sources will be found in E. HOLT, *A Documentary History of Art*, vol. II, New York, 1958, R. KLEIN and H. ZERNER, *Italian Art 1500-1600*, New Jersey, 1966, and W. STECHOW, *Northern Renaissance Art 1400-1600*, New Jersey, 1966. A. BLUNT's *Artistic Theory in Italy, 1450-1600*, Oxford, 1940, deals critically with these and other sources. The standard bibliography is the indispensable *Letteratura Artistica* by J. VON SCHLOSSER-MAGNINO, ed. O. Kurz, Florence, 1956. Most of the sixteenth-century Italian writers have been republished recently in the *Scrittori d'Italia* series.

For the historical background, the reader should turn to such books as K. D. VERNON, *Italy from 1494-1790*, Cambridge, 1909; P. BURKE, *The Renaissance*, London, 1964; D. HAY, *Italian Renaissance*, Cambridge, 1961; *The Age of the Renaissance*, ed. by D. Hay, London 1967; M. PHILLIPS, *Erasmus and the Northern Renaissance*, London, 1949; A. DICKENS, *Reformation and Society in 16th century Europe*, London, 1966; and the relevant chapters in the New Cambridge Modern History, vols. I and II, 1957 and 1962.

General histories of art include A. CHASTEL, *The Age of Humanism, 1480-1530*, London, 1963; A. BLUNT, *Art and Architecture in France, 1500-1700*, London, 1953; GEORGE KUBLER and MARTIN SORIA, *Art and Architecture in Spain and*

Portugal ... 1500-1800, London, 1959; O. BENESCH, *The Art of the Renaissance in Northern Europe*, London, 1966.

Architecture

P. LETAROUILLY, *Edifices de Rome Moderne*, 4 vols., Paris, 1840-57, and 6 vols., London, 1928-30 (excellent illustrations)

G. MASSON, *Italian Villas and Palaces*, London, 1959

P. MURRAY, *Architecture of the Italian Renaissance*, London, 1963

J. SUMMERSON, *Architecture in Britain, 1530-1830*, London, 4th ed., 1963

R. WITTKOWER, *Architectural Principles in the Age of Humanism*, London, 3rd ed., 1962

H. WÖLFFLIN, *Renaissance and Baroque*; trans. K. Simon, London, 1964

Painting and Sculpture

L. BECHERUCCI, *Manieristi Toscani*, Bergamo, 1944 (in Italian)

G. BRIGANTI, *Italian Mannerism*, London, 1962

S. J. FREEDBERG, *Painting of the High Renaissance ...*, 2 vols., Harvard, 1961

M. J. FRIEDLÄNDER, *From Van Eyck to Bruegel*, London, 1956

C. GOULD, *Introduction to Italian Renaissance Painting*, London, 1957

J. POPE-HENNESSY, *Italian High Renaissance and Baroque Sculpture*, 3 vols., London, 1963

E. K. WATERHOUSE, *Painting in Britain, 1530-1790*, London, 1953

Monographs

A fuller list will be found in PETER and LINDA MURRAY, *Dictionary of Art and Artists*, London, 1965 (hard-cover edition). For Raphael's pupils and followers the British Museum Catalogue of Italian Drawings, *Raphael and his Circle*, compiled by PHILIP POUNCEY and JOHN GERE, London, 1962, should be consulted.

Altdorfer: O. BENESCH, Vienna, 1939 and 1943 (in German)

Bronzino: A. MCCOMB, Cambridge, Mass., 1928

Bruegel: F. GROSSMANN, London (1955, in progress). For his drawings: L. MÜNZ, London, 1961; C. DE TOLNAY, London, 1952

Cellini: *Autobiography*, trans. by G. Bull, London, 1956

Cranach: E. RUHMER, London, 1963

Eworth: Catalogue of Exhibition, Leicester, 1965, and National Portrait Gallery, London, 1966

Giulio Romano: F. HARTT, 2 vols., Yale, 1958

El Greco: H. WETHEY, 2 vols., Princeton, 1962; E. DU G. TRAPIER, *El Greco's Early Years at Toledo, 1576-86*, New York, 1958

Hilliard: E. AUERBACH, London, 1961; Catalogue by G. REYNOLDS of Exhibition at Victoria and Albert Museum, London, 1947

Holbein: P. GANZ, London, 1950. For the Windsor drawings: K. PARKER, London and Oxford, 1945.

Michelangelo: C. DE TOLNAY, Princeton, 1943 (5 vols. so far); Catalogue of Drawings in the British Museum by J. WILDE, London, 1953; *Letters* trans. and ed. by E. Ramsden, 2 vols., London, 1963; C. DE TOLNAY, *Art and Thought of Michelangelo*, New York, 1964. On his architecture: J. ACKERMAN, 2 vols., London, 1961

Morales: E. DU G. TRAPIER, New York, 1933; I. BÄCKSBACKA, Helsinki, 1962 (in English)

Oliver: Catalogue by G. REYNOLDS of Exhibition at Victoria and Albert Museum, London, 1947

Philibert de l'Orme: A. BLUNT, London, 1958

Palladio: J. ACKERMAN, London, 1966

Parmigianino: S. J. FREEDBERG, Cambridge, Mass., 1950. For his drawings: A. E. POPHAM, London, 1953

Pontormo: F. CLAPP, Yale, 1916. For his drawings: J. C. REARICK, 2 vols., Harvard, 1964

Primaticcio: L. DIMIER, Paris, 1928 (in French)

Rosso: K. KUSENBERG, Paris, 1931 (in French); Catalogue of the Pontormo Exhibition, Florence, 1956

Sanmicheli: E. LANGENSKIÖLD, London, 1938; Catalogue of the Sanmicheli Exhibition, Verona, 1960

Smythson: M. GIROUARD, London, 1966

Tintoretto: H. TIETZE, London, 1948

Vasari: R. CARDEN, London, 1910; E. RUD, London, 1964. For eds. of the *Lives*, which include his *Autobiography*, see under SOURCES

Veronese: A. ORLIAC, London, 1948

List of Illustrations

Entries are listed alphabetically under the names of artists. Measurements are given in centimetres. Plate numbers in bold type indicate colour illustrations.

209

Index

213